AF267383

# The seven Laws of Reality and Being

## A manual about the Seven Hermetic Principles which govern reality and phenomena

# The seven Laws of Reality and Being

A manual about the Seven Hermetic Principles which govern reality and phenomena

## Max Corradi

Jaborandi Publishing

Text copyright: Max Corradi 2013
Second Edition 2023

Full cover image artwork by the artist Cristina Jimenez Rodriguez
Contact: kristinajr.cristina@gmail.com


Jaborandi Publishing 2013
All rights reserved

The rights of Max Corradi as author have been asserted in
accordance with the Copyright, Designs and Patents Act 1988

Other books by the author:

Cures without side effects
"Practical healing manual of the most essential and effective
biotherapy treatments"
Jaborandi Publishing

Low dose medicine
"Healing without side effects using low dose cytokines,
interleukins, hormones, and neurotrophines"
Jaborandi Publishing

Healing with Micotherapy
"Self-Healing with therapeutic mushrooms"
Jaborandi Publishing

No Age Ontology
"The Joy of Timelessness"
Jaborandi Publishing

# Table of Contents

This book is dedicated to all my kind Teachers and all
those who are seeking

*"The lips of Wisdom are closed, except to the ears of Understanding."*

*The Kybalion*

## Summary and intent of the whole book

Reality, the Universe, God, events and circumstances are Mind, all beings are Mind, and **Mind is Reality, an all pervading mirror-like lucid Awareness of Pure Being.** Reality, Mind and individual beings are non-dual. Sentient beings are at the same time individual and indivisible from each other and the totality of Pure Being, the nature of Reality. Since this is so, you, as an all pervading lucid Awareness 'unconsciously' or 'unknowingly' think, talk and act everything into being in your field of experience which is your life. Once this is understood and, above all, realized, you can consciously and intentionally think, talk and act everything which serves you and others into the field of experience of your life. Eventually and ultimately, by realizing that you are Mind, Reality, an all pervading mirror-like lucid Awareness as an ongoing uninterrupted experience, you will know the 'Truth that sets you free', from illusion-like birth and death, suffering and frustration.

*"Reality, life, existence is like a play or a game, but if you don't know the rules it can and does easily turn into the worst nightmare"*

*Anonymous*

# Important disclaimer

Reality, Pure Being, Mind, God or Bhraman, Buddha or Enlightenment cannot be explained through words, concepts or ideas, and its realization cannot be transferred from one being to another being; each sentient being has to realize Reality, Pure Being as his own experience and until such a personal realization, and as long as one grasps at a seeming duality of subject and object, there will always be an underlining experience of dissatisfaction, frustration and suffering.

But if one wants to attempt to explain Reality, the closest explanation that conceptual mind can comprehend is 'like' this:

Reality, Pure Being, Mind, all pervading Awareness of Pure Being, God or Buddha, is an absolute totality or non-duality where all things, events, meanings and every sentient being with a consciousness, whether it be an animal, human, ghost, demon, god, angel, saint, archangel, is not separate from the totality of the play of this very Reality; but, at the same time and without contradiction, each one is a complete separate individual sentient being capable of realizing himself or herself as this Reality of Pure Being, the totality of all events and meanings, or, otherwise, by not realizing his/her identity with Reality, each separate individual living being is capable of producing an individually limited reality which unfolds according to precise and unchangeable Laws.

This individual limited reality is then shared with other beings with a similar conditioned, limited or 'periscopic' mindset through these same Laws. From infinite Timeless, identityless and all-pervading Pure Being one ends up as a sentient being imprisoned by all dualities, dualistic concepts and with dualistic intentions and aims with all their infinite consequences. From Timeless all-pervading Awareness one ends up as the limited awareness of dualistic consciousness.

Since all things and all sentient beings are included, non-separate and non-dual as the 'One Reality', it's tempting to say that 'we are all one' or 'we are all part of the One' and nothing and nobody exists at all apart from the One, Reality, Pure Being or God. But, at the same time and without contradiction, because Reality, spontaneously and without intention to do so, expresses itself continuously as a play or a dance of individual forms and events, it is also tempting to say that everything, each and every living being, is a separate and autonomous being with a self-identity of its own.

Realization, Enlightenment, Awakening or 'knowledge of God' is 'like' breaking all the logical conceptual chains that affirm that these two separate modes of being cannot be integrated, or gone beyond in the one only concept-less experience of Reality, Pure Being, Mind as all-pervading Awareness, immanent and, at the same time and without any contradiction, transcendent of all phenomena.

The real nature of every individual and seemingly separate sentient being, is the potentiality of all possible events and meanings, and, at the same time and without contradiction, a completely free individuality capable of either recognizing or not recognizing itself as this potentiality of all pervading Awareness of Pure Being. One's only real duty in life is to discover first, then familiarize oneself and finally realize that one is identical with Pure Being, that one is Reality, the one 'Truth that will set you free'.


**Nobody owns Reality**
**Anybody can realize Reality**
**Nobody owns the Truth**
**Anybody can realize the Truth**
**Knowledge overcomes all fears**


*"There is no Truth in any concept of Truth".*

*Saraha (8th century CE)*

I pay homage to Pure Being, Reality itself, and all the great Teachers and Holders of Knowledge who abide within the Reality of Pure Being, the lions of speech which manifest in existence for the benefit of all. May the flame of excellent Knowledge burn all doubts and confusion and bring infinite absolute and relative joy to all beings.

*Purum Esse Sustantia Omnium Rerum Est*

# Introduction

*"The Principles of Truth are Seven; he who knows these, understandingly, possesses the Magic Key before whose touch all the doors of the Temple fly open."*

*The Kybalion*

This book is mainly based on the seven Hermetic Principles of Reality and Being which can be employed in order to change one's life conditions and circumstances as explained in the Hermetic book *"The Kybalion: A Study of the Hermetic Philosophy of Ancient Egypt and Greece"* published in 1908 and authored by 'Three Initiates' often identified as the New Thought pioneer William Walker Atkinson (1862–1932).

These seven Laws of Reality can be regarded as the essential Principles of all the Western and Eastern spiritual and non-spiritual Wisdom traditions, and this is this reason why this book also draws many parallelisms with all these different traditions and teachings, not with the intention to mix up the different subtle differences between the various Wisdom traditions in a kind of 'minestrone soup', but on the contrary, **in order to clarify and show how different conceptual paths try to lead the individual to the one and only non-conceptual experience of Reality directly or indirectly according to the different mindsets and beliefs of the beings in different time periods and cultures.**

In final analysis, Truth is always found to be the same whether stated in modern scientific terms or in the language of ancient religion or philosophy, the only difference being in the form of presentation, always bearing in mind that no human formula will ever be able to describe every side of it.

This is not to say that all paths and traditions lead to the experience and realization of Reality, **but that all paths and spiritual traditions forged upon the realization of Reality lead to the experience and realization of Reality using different symbols, concepts and words that fit with a specific culture, time and place.**

Hermes Trimegistus (the three times great Hermes), from which the word 'Hermetic' in the title derives, was the Greek god or personification of Wisdom equivalent to the ancient Egyptian god 'Thoth', and the Buddhist manifestation of Wisdom 'Manjushri'.

The dates of his last incarnation on earth are not known, but presumably they can be fixed in the early days of the oldest dynasties of Egypt, long before the days of Moses. Some authorities regard him as a contemporary of Abraham, and some Jewish traditions claim that Abraham acquired a portion of his mystical knowledge from Hermes himself. Although the name Hermes does not appear in the Qur'an, early Islamic hagiographers and chroniclers identified Hermes Trismegistus with Idris, whom the Arabs also identified with Enoch. Idris or Hermes was termed 'The three times Wise'.

**But in real sense Hermes is Wisdom itself, and thus anything written through the inspiration of true Wisdom is in reality written by Hermes, Thoth, Idris or Manjushri. The personage or 'personalness' behind is irrelevant.**

In the history of humanity on earth true Hermetic knowledge has been transmitted, all the way through the ages, most of the time secretly, and many have been the holders and adepts which manifested this knowledge, not only in the Eastern and Western spiritual traditions but often as 'ordinary' lay people involved in arts, literature, politics and science. An example of this in the West are figures like Paracelsus, Leonardo Da Vinci, Galileo, Dante Alighieri, Marsilio Ficino, Isaac Newton, William Shakespeare, Giordano Bruno, Cornelius Agrippa, William Blake, William Walker Atkinson, Thomas Troward and Albert Einstein to name only a few.

In the East, on the other hand, there have been many spiritual adepts or Teachers from the Buddhist, Hindu, and Tao traditions of Knowledge that have realized the Truth of Mind and its Principles.

**The Hermetic tradition in particular speaks of seven Hermetic Principles, seven Laws or Principles which govern Reality and Being.** These are unchangeable Laws like the physical law of gravity, but unlike the law of gravity they apply to all the different levels of Reality, (mind, energy and physical level). **These Seven Principles were expanded and commented by the great**

Hermetic scholar and metaphysician William Walker Atkinson in the book *'The Kybalion'* which I quote at the beginning of each chapter.

The Seven Hermetic Laws of Reality are not exclusive of each other, in the same way as the law of gravity is not exclusive of the law of lift on the physical plane, **but work in synergy to shape the minds and phenomena of infinite sentient beings and their environments.**

In practical terms we can use any law of nature, but we cannot alter it. For example, we can use the law of gravity and the law of lift and fly through the sky, but if we jumped off a cliff, gravity would pull us down and we would injure ourselves and die. Therefore we can understand that by opposing any natural law we place ourselves in an inverted position with regard to the law itself, and therefore, it appears as though the law itself is working against us with a definite purpose, where in real sense this inversion is entirely caused by ourselves, **by our ignorance of the law and not from any change in the action of the law.**

**This is the reasons why in theistic religions one often finds the concept of God's punishment, where the real meaning behind it is only one's ignorance and the subsequent inverted position in regard to the these unchangeable Laws of  Reality.** On the other hand, if one has knowledge of these laws one can use them at one's own advantage by using skillful methods,  which will be explained in part two of the book, and achieve new life conditions and fulfillment.

In relation to this, although in part one very  profound concepts regarding Reality, the Universe and Being are explained in a very simple and straightforward style, some readers might be tempted to skip and  jump directly to the more practical methods presented in part two. But in fact, in connection with the methods described part two, while anyone may obtain some degree of success by practicing them alone, still in order to obtain any marked degree of success **it is necessary to have first reflected, understood and realized the main principles concerning Mind and the Seven Principles of Reality as a whole.** Hoverer, by studying, reflecting and making use of the skillful methods outlined in chapter eight, new life conditions such as a healthier, calmer, joyful and more fulfilling life experience can be achieved.

**The seven Hermetic Laws or Principles which govern Reality are:**

    I.    **The Principle of Mind (All is Mind)**
    II.    **The Principle of Cause and Effect**
    III.    **The Principle of Vibration or Sound**
    IV.    **The Principle of Correspondence**
    V.    **The Principle of Polarity or Opposites**
    VI.    **The Principle of Rhythm or Cyclicity**
    VII.    **The Principle of Gender**

The first Principle of Mind could be said to represent 'the Absolute' aspect of Reality transcendent and immanent at the same time. The other six principles represent the way in which this Mind Principle manifests as 'the relative', **although in actual fact both the absolute and the relative are indivisible as non-dual Reality itself.**

Note: Throughout the book I will use the terms Mind, Fundamental Mind, Universal Mind, Nature of Mind, Reality, all pervading lucid Awareness, Spirit, Pure Being, and Wisdom interchangeably as their intended meaning is the same. I will also use the terms Reality, Pure Being and Mind in capital letter to mean the potentiality of the all-pervading Awareness of Pure Being. On the other hand I will use the terms reality, mind, dualistic mind, limited awareness, consciousness or dualistic consciousness in small letter to mean exclusively Mind's relative limited manifestations in time and space.

*He, who has ears to hear, let him hear."*

*Matthew 13:9*

# Part 1

# The seven Hermetic Principles of Reality

# Chapter 1

# The Principle of Mind

*"The All is Mind; The Universe is Mental."*

*The Kybalion*

## The Principle of Mind

**The first Hermetic Principle says that everything, from the The first Hermetic Principle says that everything, from the whole material universe, its energy, the phenomena of life and all the different sentient beings contained therein are nothing other than Mind, Pure Being, an all pervading Awareness.**

This is an infinite and eternal energy, 'mentative' in its nature, **out of and in which** all things are evolved manifestations. All is Mind, and all is in Mind, all things are centers of mental activity and energy, in the Great Universal Ocean of Mind Energy which is infinitely individualized. What is generally known as Spirit or God in the West is also the uncreated Principle of Mind.

Sometimes this Mind is called 'all-pervading ocean of Mind power' because it contains within itself all the power, and energy that there is. It is the source from which all forms of energy and matter arise. Sometimes it is called 'infinite living Mind' because we cannot fully describe it and it is the source of all life. **It can also be defined as infinite all-pervading uncreated Awareness of Pure Being.**

According to the Hermetic tradition Reality is an absolute unity; it is a state of total liberty, whole, complete, and perfect as it is, without a cause, infinite and beyond time and space, formless, indivisible and immutable, immanent and transcendent without contradiction. Reality can also be defined as infinite substance, infinite play of energy, and infinite play of life, infinite law, infinite love, and infinite Mind.

Mind creates spontaneous, it is the unconditioned and absolute ground for all that exists. In itself it is 'all that is', in its creation it is 'all that appears'.

**The Universe, including sentient beings, is manifested in and by infinite all pervasive uncreated and uncompounded Mind, and since the creator and its creations are of the same nature, sentient beings are of the same nature as all pervasive Mind.** Moreover, since Mind is immanent in its creation, at the heart of every conscious sentient being there is the Presence and Potentiality of Pure Being. **As the Ground or potentiality of all that appears, Mind is beyond any Laws, but its manifestation is governed by unchanging Laws.**

The spontaneous Will of Reality is universal energy, the pure logic of Reality is universal Law, and the essence of Reality is universal Life. There is nothing in the universe which is about 'non-being', the whole multidimensional universe is thriving with life and unending Being. The Principle of Reality always remains itself without any changes, indivisible and immutable, and, likewise, each sentient being is identical with it in the totality of its essence, nature, and substance.

Reality, Mind can also be described using the three aspects of the potential, the ideal and the concrete. The potential is Pure Being itself, Mind's potentiality not particularized in any way, not yet brought into form nor thought. The ideal is the particularizing of the potential into a certain spontaneous manifestation beyond or within time and space. The concrete is the physical manifestation within space and time in visible form.

**One should not think as Mind as one creator separate from sentient beings, because each sentient being is the whole of Reality for himself. Mind is infinitely individualized in each sentient being.**

## Mind's generic character

**Now we come to the generic character of this universal Mind power, which can be summed up in the words *'Total Unchanging Goodness'* beyond the relative conflicting concepts of good and evil.**

Whether one is a human being, an animal, a ghost, an angel or a demon, one's Fundamental Mind of Pure Being does not change in any way, it is and it remains a *'Total Unchanging Goodness'* beyond the relative conflicting concepts of good and evil. Its generic tendency or expressive power is always toward more life, wisdom, love, and liberty both in generic and individual terms.

**Since it is a universal principle it can have no particular interests to serve, and therefore its activities are always equal.** For this reason on the relative level the positive pole, being closer to its essential principle, always overcomes the negative pole. Just as water, electricity, or any other physical force will not work contrary to its generic character, Mind will not work contrary to its generic character, nevertheless one can so easily place oneself in an inverted position in regard to it, and, therefore, even though it appears as the principle itself is working against oneself with a definite purpose, **this inversion is entirely caused by the individual, and not from any change in the generic character of the principle.**

In a nutshell, it's not the generic character of the all-pervasive Mind which creates strife in the world **but the inherent freedom of 'forgetfulness' within Mind that allows each individualized Mind- being to not recognize his identity with Mind and therefore to place himself or herself in an inverted position in regard to Mind's generic character** followed by the subsequent suffering that it entails which manifest through the relative Laws of Reality.

The Principle of all pervading Mind and the fact that one is always the center of this infinite play of Reality for oneself accounts for all the claims that have ever been made for the creative power of one's intentional thoughts over phenomena.

The reason lies in the fact that each being is the center of the Universe as one's appearances made up of 'Mind stuff', and therefore one has the power, by directing one's own intentions, thoughts and emotional energy, to control or shape all things contained. **If the Universe is in essence a manifestation of all pervasive Mind and therefore made up of 'Mind stuff', then Mind must have the highest power over its phenomena.** This is why without some degree of understanding of this first principle, all the methods explained in chapter eight will work only to a minor degree.

## God, Being in the Judeo - Christian tradition

*"For in him we live and move and have our being'"*

*Acts 17:28*

In the book of Exodus, God commands Moses to tell the people that **'the One who is'** has sent him. The original four letters expressing the name of God are  הוהי  transliterated as the Latin letters 'YHWH', most likely pronounced 'Yahweh' and are derived from a verb that means 'to be', so the most likely translation would be **'the One who is'**. Grammar tells us that the verb 'to be' is a substantive verb, that is, belonging to the real or essential nature of a thing, therefore it does not indicate any action passing from the subject to an object. **This being so, when we come to examine the nature, attributes and qualities of 'Pure Being', we are forced to use the term potentiality instead of actuality.** Although the most accurate translation of the name of God would simply be **'Being' or 'the One who is',** since this principle is always individualized, in the sense that we need someone to express it, **many spiritual teachings use the term 'I AM'. 'I' because it is individualized but at the same time identityless (without any identity, not a separate being out there), 'Am' because it is always in a state of Being beyond all dualities of birth and death.**

This should also not cause the confusion of identifying the name of God with some self-entity external to the play of Reality but on the contrary we should understand God, as the fundamental Expanse of Pure Being, or **'Pure Beingness'**, a mirror-like all pervading Awareness beyond the limitation of external or internal, one or many, time and space **residing at the heart of each sentient being.** From this substantive pure potentiality there flows out an active verb, which reproduces in action, what the 'I AM' is in essence, **creation is in essence the same as what has started the creation.**

On the other hand, the devil in its general aspect is the possibility of not recognizing one's identity with 'the One who is' (God), **straying into dualism and the grasping at duality of subject and object.** In its individual aspect the devil is **the personification and symbol of sentient beings dualistic limitations due to not knowing their identity with Mind of Pure Being and all the negative intentions and actions that sprout because of that limitation:** in a nutshell the devil is 'conceptual limitations'. Its number, the triple six spoken of in the Bible, is the repetition (dualism) of the three indivisible aspects of Pure Being and Reality:  the Father, the Holy Spirit and the Son, or the Potential, the Ideal and the Concrete or the Essence, the Nature and the Responsiveness.

**In summary, God is the selfless and Timeless Presence of 'the One who is', an individualized essence of mirror-like Awareness of Pure Being, beyond subject and object or gender residing at the heart of each manifested sentient being whether it be a god, human, animal, spirit, angel, or demon. This mirror-like all pervading Awareness of Pure Being is capable of reflecting or manifesting itself into infinite forms, endowed with the capacity of recognizing or 'forgetting' its own source as Pure Being.**

*"Look inside of you, Sagredo, listen to your internal voice and remember that the true Teacher is Pure Being which whispers inside of yourself. Please listen to it: it is the Truth which is in you. You are divine, never forget this! We are not separating Sagredo, separation*

*does not exist, we are all one in eternal contact with the Unique Soul.."*

Giordano Bruno last testament before being burnt alive by the inquisition in February 1600

## God, Pure Consciousness and the Self in the Hindu tradition

Although there are many interpretations and philosophical views in the Hindu spiritual tradition, we can consider the words of Sri Ramana Maharshi, an Indian Teacher or Swami who lived and taught in south India in the early part of the 20$^{th}$ century, one of the most essential and profound in describing Reality (God) and Wisdom **according to the Advaita Vedanta (non-dual) Hindu tradition.**

**According to Sri Ramana Maharshi, the term 'God', 'Self' or 'Brahman' used in the Hindu tradition are synonyms with Reality which is discovered by Self-Realization.** Therefore realization of the Self is realization of God, **but it is not an experience of God, rather it is an understanding that oneself is indivisible from God.** Speaking from this ultimate level, Sri Ramana Maharshi's statements on God can be summarized in three main points:

- God is immanent and formless, pure or essential Being and pure Consciousness.
- Manifestations appear in God and through God's power, but God is not its creator. God never acts intentionally as God possesses neither a self, nor a will or a desire to act; God just is as it is.
- God's Individuality is the illusion that we are not identical with God; when the illusion is dispelled, what remains is God.

Sri Ramana Maharshi speaks also about 'Iswara', the Hindu name for the supreme *personified* God of worship. He says that Iswara exists as a real entity only as long as one imagines that one is a separate identified being. **When identity persists there is a God who survives the activities of the Universe, in the absence of identity the concept of 'Iswara' is non-existent.** Also beside Iswara, Hinduism has many deities which resemble the gods and demons of Greek mythology. Such deities are a central feature of popular Hinduism and their reality is still widely accepted. **Sri Ramana Maharshi claims that such beings are as real as the people who believe in them.** He admits that after realization they share the same fate as Iswara, as being unreal and identical with God, but prior to that, he regards them as important beings in a cosmological hierarchy which can affect the world in same way.

To sum up, in the Hindu Advaita Vedanta Wisdom tradition **'Brahman' (Reality, not to be confused with the deity 'Brahmā')** cannot be known as an object of mind because Brahman is one's very Mind, moreover the goal of Vedanta is to realize that one's self (atman) is a product of ego false-identification when in reality, Brahman is all that exists; which leads to the conclusion that we are all ultimately Brahman.

**Therefore it may be said that Self-Liberation or Enlightenment does not merely mean to know Brahman, but rather to realize one's 'Brahman-hood', to actually realize that one is and always was Brahman.**

# The principle of 'Mind Only' in the Buddhist tradition

*"In a mirror surface or the surface of a vessel, a woman, as she adorns herself, sees her face, though her entire face seems to appear in these, it is neither existent nor non-existent there. All phenomena should be known to be like that".*

*The Buddha - Shri Samadhiraja Sutra*

In the Mahayana Buddhist tradition we find a particular doctrine called 'Mind Only' (Chittamatra) or 'The Doctrine of Consciousness' (Vijnanavada). **The 'Mind Only' tenet system asserts that there are no such things as external phenomena. Mind, as a non-dual self-aware consciousness, is an absolute Reality.** It is founded upon the Buddha's statement that **"*All three worlds are mind only*"** and it is expressed mainly in Buddhist scriptures  like the 'Lankavatara' and 'Dasabhumika' Sutra.

In the visual cognition of the visual form of a table, the visual form and the visual consciousness seeing it come from or share the same source, **a karmic ground**. They arise simultaneously from it as parts of a single cognition, without coming from different sources. The great Buddhist 'Mind Only' Teacher Asanga in one of his works says that it is awareness (mind) which arises  in  the appearance of external objects, living beings, identities, and sense-data.

Thus  it  is  nothing  but  consciousness or mind  itself  that appears  externally  to  be things and living beings, and internally to be a self-perceiving entity, and since objects which  appear  to be 'out there'  are  nothing  but  mind  itself, **what we regard as reality is an illusory manifestation of mind itself.** Another important feature of this system is the concept of the eight types or aspects of consciousness.

**These eight types of consciousness should be understood as different aspects of the mind or consciousness of an ordinary sentient being and not as separate unconnected entities, although their function in shaping our 'external and internal reality' is different.**

In general the Buddhist scriptures talk of five aspects of consciousness, five sensory consciousnesses, plus a mental consciousness. But in the Mind Only school two more aspects of consciousness are added to the five: the afflicted mind consciousness and the store-house or ground consciousness.

**The five sense consciousnesses** arise in conjunction with the five physical sense faculties, and the sixth consciousness, arises in conjunction with the faculty of the conscious mind.

**The sixth consciousness** is also called 'the intermediate consciousness' or the consciousness following immediately upon arising of sense perception. As soon as a sensory perception such as form occurs, the mental concept of that form immediately arises. The sixth mental consciousness, like the sensory consciousnesses, it exists in one instant and ceases in the next moment.

**The seventh consciousness**, the afflicted mind consciousness or ego-consciousness, is the ego principle itself, the principle of self-individuation or self-grasping at self-identity. It is called the afflicted-mind consciousness because it believes and grasps at one's own personality as a concrete self entity, thinking there is a separate 'me' or an 'I'. It possesses pride, which believes the 'I' is superior to others 'I', it has attachment to the 'I' believing oneself as more deserving than others and gives rise to all the deluded and destructive views about Reality.

**The eighth consciousness**, the store-house or ground consciousness is the source of all the other kinds of consciousness. It is beyond a subject-object duality, it is momentary and non-substantial but is not a passively receiving 'dust bin' of the mind, on the contrary it is dynamic in organizing, integrating new tendencies and structuring the individual's experience of reality, in fact it is the source of all illusory appearances of a living being.

Every sentient being with its 'seemingly subjective and objective' world can be reduced to its 'own' ground consciousness, and this ground consciousness is basically the sum of all motivated actions and intentions from beginning-less time.

The eighth consciousness, is also called the store-house consciousness because it functions as a receptacle and container of the so called 'seeds' or karmic causes of past experiences. These 'seeds' project themselves as an illusionary world of empirical subjects and corresponding objects. The ground consciousness is the foundation and source for the mind because all karmic latencies are stored in it. The latent karmic imprints settle in the ground consciousness to express themselves at a later time.

**A karmic latency will awaken as an experience of suffering or happiness when the right circumstances present themselves.** Positive karma doesn't immediately express itself as happiness, rather the karmic latencies rest within the ground consciousness and arise later as a result when the secondary circumstances allow it. Similarly, accumulated negative karma does not express itself immediately, but the karmic imprints remain in the ground consciousness to ripen under the appropriate circumstances causing suffering later on in one's experience.

All the karmic seeds, good or bad, within the ground consciousness, sprout and manifest as the other seven consciousnesses, as if the ground consciousness were the ocean and the other seven consciousnesses were waves that appear upon its surface. Since the eighth consciousness is the basis of all un-awakened experiences including future experiences, creating imprints in the present through mind training and habituation leads to experiencing their results in the future.

**Habituating oneself to positive thoughts and actions allows negative imprints to decrease and positive qualities to increase resulting in future happiness.** As we will see later in chapter eight, since the subconscious mind spoken of in Hermetic teachings is basically the eighth consciousness of the Buddhist Mind Only tradition, by working with one's conscious mind one can re-program one's subconscious mind in order to achieve new life conditions and experiences.

To conclude, the  final aim of the follower of the Buddhist 'Mind Only' school is to put an end to the tendency of external projections of the ground consciousness transforming  it into the non-dual Wisdom of Enlightened Mind, Reality itself beyond the duality of subject and object.

In the Buddhist  'Abhisamayalankara Sutra' (The Ornament of Clear Realization) we find the following statements pointing to the realization of Mind and Reality:

*"There is nothing to clear away, and nothing to be established. Reality views Reality. To see that is liberation"*

From the Buddhist Sutra Requested by the future Buddha Maitreya:

*"Mind has no shape. It has no color. It has no existence. It is like space".*

And from the 'Lankavatara Sutra':

*"Though reflections may appear within a mirror, they do not exist; and if we do not know the appearances of mind as mere appearances, the duality of conceptual thinking will arise".*

From 'Distinguishing Phenomena and Pure Being' by the future Buddha Maitreya:

*"Since experience of every phenomenon is equivalent to the center of open space, (manifesting) formations are all appearances like illusions".*

In the commentary to the same text by the Tibetan Teacher Mipham Rinpoche we find the following statement:

*"What are being called 'outer objects observed in common' are not referents existing as something extrinsic to or other than consciousness, precisely because they are appearances comprising common experiences shared by a variety of beings whose mindstreams are not the same. But this is what proves that they are nothing other than differing perceptions of differing mindstreams."*
        *"Similarly, for creatures whose operative habitual tendencies correspond, not only will environments and so on have a similar*

*appearance for as long as the energy of those habitual  tendencies has not been exhausted, but, what is more, the specific cause for their appearing to be similar will not be the existence of a referent on the outside. Just as something which one type of being sees as water will be seen as existing under another appearance by others among the six types of beings whose karmic impressions differ, anything perceived should be understood to be neither more nor less than a self-manifestation of the mentality internal to a specific observer".*

## The Mind Principle in the Tibetan Buddhist Teaching of 'Dzogchen'

*"Mind is the universal seed. Both Samsara and Nirvana spring forth from it"*

*Saraha (8th century CE)*

It is in the Tibetan Buddhist tradition, in the cycle of teachings called 'Dzogchen' that we find the most accurate and profound explanation and description of the Principle of Mind and Reality. **The term  'Dzogchen' means 'Total Perfection' or 'Total Completeness' and it refers to the true nature of Reality, phenomena and of each individual sentient being as totally perfect and complete as it is.**

In the cycle of Dzogchen teachings called 'the category of Mind' (Semde) a refutation is made that the eight aspects of consciousness and the whole universe, or appearances of the Mind are Mind, **because a more precise assertion is made that appearances and phenomena are the *projections or self-manifested reflections* of the Nature of Mind (or Mind Principle), similar to various reflections appearing on a polished and lucid mirror, where the mirror symbolizes the Nature of Mind's infinite potentiality to manifest an array of forms and events, and where the  reflections cannot be said to be the mirror itself, but neither  separate from the mirror in which  they appear.**

In this tradition, Mind is called the 'Nature of Mind' or the 'Primordial State' or the 'Vast Expanse of unconditioned Primordial Space and Awareness' similar to the potentiality of the lucid surface of a mirror, and Mind's manifestations comprising all the eight aspects of consciousness are simply called mind, dualistic mind, consciousness or limited awareness, similar to the reflections manifesting on a mirror's surface.

The Primordial State, the 'Vast Expanse of unconditioned primordial Space and Awareness' is the root and real nature of the phenomenal Universe and of each individual sentient being and not an abstract concept. **Within and by the Primordial Ground of Pure Being, the Nature of Mind, an array of illusory forms are self-manifested as a spontaneous play of effulgence, at which point two possibilities open up**: either self-recognition as self-manifestation beyond all opposites, and therefore the possibility to freely be directly aware of  this infinite play of creation non dualistically (without the illusory division of subject and object, time and space), or otherwise, non recognition and the subsequent forming of tightly grasped dualistic concepts of opposite values.

In the first case one is Self-Awakened into the totality of the Primordially Pure Ground of Being, free, but at the same time, master of time and space; **in the second case one is trapped into the illusory nature of dualistic values of one's now 'limited dualistic awareness',** including time and space, until one 're-Awakens' through a spiritual path into the self-recognition of oneself as the primordially Pure Ground of Being which now is called the fruit of Self Awakening or Enlightenment.

In Dzogchen, the mirror symbolizes the potentiality of the Nature of Mind to manifest, and the images and forms reflected symbolize the various manifestations or appearances of the five senses, plus thoughts and emotions which can be said to be the 'objects' of consciousness. Moreover in Dzogchen a clear distinction is made between the non-dual and all-pervading Awareness of Enlightened experience, which is a pure, timeless, unborn potentiality of total knowing (Awareness), and the identified limited dualistic consciousness characteristic of a sentient being.

**In the Dzogchen teachings the Mind and the eight aspects of consciousness are not the same thing but also not separate entities either, in fact the eight aspects of consciousness are 'reflections' or manifestations of the radiant effulgence of the intrinsic Nature of Mind, just like the rays of the sun are not the sun itself but also cannot be separated from the sun.**

One could say that consciousness has its root in Mind, or that mind has its root in the Nature of Mind, and the intended meaning would be the same. Realization of the Nature of Mind and dualistic consciousness (self-grasping mind) are not mutually exclusive either, since consciousness has its root and is embraced (or contained in) by the Nature of Mind as its spontaneous play, just like the reflections in the mirror are 'embraced' and are not separate from the mirror itself.

**Just like one needs reflections to discover the potentiality, nature, quality and attributes of a mirror, when one is on the Dzogchen Path to self-realization, one can use any of the Mind's spontaneous effulgent reflections to discover the potentiality and nature of the source of Pure Being** which is manifesting and reflecting, therefore one can use mind or consciousness (emotions, passions, or any type of experienced phenomena) to discover one's Nature of Mind of Pure Being.

While in the Dzogchen path one 'jumps' directly into one's nature of Pure Being and integrates all dualistic experiences in that state, in the Buddhist higher path of Tantric transformation, one uses precise symbols in the form of Awakened Deities (equivalent to the mirror's reflections) to discover and abide in the nature of the potentiality of Pure Being which is reflecting (equivalent to the mirror's lucid surface potentiality).

The Nature of Mind is described as primordially pure, all pervasive, uncompounded and without characteristics but, at the same time, possessing an infinite potentiality to manifest as pure or impure phenomena (i.e. Buddhas or sentient beings) **simply depending on whether it recognizes itself or not as the source of its effulgent manifestation.**

Just like a mirror doesn't have any plans or intention to reflect but it is just part of its potentiality to reflect when objects and circumstances present themselves, the all-pervasive Mind, mirror-like Awareness in its essence, nature and responsiveness manifest forms and appearances only when and if secondary causes and circumstances present themselves.

**Moreover, just as the surface of the mirror is not affected by its good or bad reflections, whether one is a human being, an animal, a ghost, an angel or a demon, one's fundamental Mind of Pure Being, mirror-like all pervading Awareness does not change and it cannot be modified or improved in any way, it is beyond the Principle of Cause and Effect and it cannot be polluted by any emotions, thoughts, intentions or actions whether they be positive or negative.**

The '*All Knowing*' Longchen Rabjam, a 14th century Tibetan Teacher who is considered an incarnation or supreme manifestation of Enlightened Wisdom 'Manjushri', elucidates in the '*Shingta Chenpo*' a commentary of one of his treatises called '*Relaxation in the nature of Mind*', the relation between Mind and appearance of Mind like this[1]:

*"Although forms appear to the Mind, the objective appearances are not Mind …when the reflection of your face appears in a mirror, it appears as the face looks, because the clear surface of the mirror is capable of making the reflection appear and the face has the potential of appearing or of projecting the reflection. At that time, the reflection of the face is not the face, nor is there any other face than the face which imprinted it. Likewise, various kinds of phenomena are appearing to the deluded mind because of the interdependent origination of the causes and conditions of delusion. …The various objective appearances are not mind, because the objects remain even when the person himself is not there. The objects won't move when the person moves elsewhere; and the objects possess various colors and so on.*

*If the objects are the mind itself then they should change as the mind changes, they should be present if it is present, and if it is not, they shouldn't be. As mind has no color and design, neither should*

---

[1] From "The practice of Dzogchen", Longhen Rabjam, translated by Tulku Thondup. Snow Lion publication.

*the objects have them. The presence and absence of appearance are the projections of the mind. So the mere appearance can be classified as the mind....The reflections appear in a mirror without the face passing into the mirror, nor do the reflections occur separately from the face. Likewise it should be understood that from the very moment that all phenomena appear in the mind, they exist neither as the mind nor as anything other than the mind."*

And from the same text:

*" Though by the force of habitual patterns, there appears, the dualistic appearance of grasping and fixation, from the time they appear the grasper and grasped have not been two, this is like a face reflected in a mirror...*

*...These phenomena, the phenomenal world of Samsara and Nirvana, do indeed appear, but from the time they appear, they do not exist as anything external, internal, or in between."*

In the above sentence *'so the mere appearance can be classified as the mind'* and in other treatises Longchen Rabjam explains and interprets the common assertion that **appearances are mind as just a common way of speaking, like one would  say that the rays of the sun are the sun or the waves of the ocean are the ocean.**
The spontaneous radiations or manifestations of the Nature of Mind (uncompounded all-pervading Awareness) as various appearances, forms, sounds, emotions and dualistic consciousness are pervaded or imbued by and with the lucid Primordial Awareness of the Ground of Being, therefore we can find the common assertion that 'appearances are Awareness', or 'appearances are mind'.

The three times of past, present and future are contained evenly  in the single all-pervading Awareness of the Nature of Mind, the pure and spontaneously manifesting Primordial State of any individual sentient being.

From the Dzochen Semde Tantra Text the 'All creating King'[2]:

*"The three times are a single one without distinction. Arising is primordial, with neither before nor after. Because Reality is one and completely all-pervading, one rests within the nature of the greatest of the great."*

*"Without remainder all phenomena, however they appear, are emanated by mind, produced by the Nature of Mind".*

*And:*

*"When the nature of me, the doer of all, is not realized, the phenomena created by me are imputed with fixed existence. By the power of attachment and craving, apparent things exist. And so their impermanent nature as illusion is destroyed".*

From the same source:

*"Both the environment and the inhabitants, Buddhas and sentient beings, all the phenomenal world were made by Mind, and they are one within the Mind."*

...

*"Within the unborn, in Dharmata (the Nature of Reality) completely pure, the appearance of things that are born rises like a reflection."*

Just like a mirror would be useless if it didn't perform the function of reflecting forms, **the Primordial State recognizes itself through and by its own self reflecting effulgence,** in which case there is the permanent Awakening as a Buddha or an Awakened One, the non-dual totality of all events and meanings.

---

[2] Cited by Longchen Rabjam, in the 'Shingta Chenpo' a commentary of one of his treatises called 'Relaxation in the nature of Mind'.

On the other hand, **Mind also possesses the intrinsic freedom to not recognize its own self reflected manifestations,** and in which case there is the phenomenon of birth into an illusory, and potentially infinite, number of sentient beings until re-Awakening is actualized through a specific spiritual path.

To conclude, beside the mirror, sometimes the symbol of the crystal is used in Dzogchen Teaching. In this case the clear, pure and limpid crystal symbolizes one's state of Pure Being in its aspect of pure potentiality and with its spontaneous radiant effulgence not yet manifested, and the light of sun symbolizing the secondary causes activating the crystal's manifestation of light colors in space as its spontaneous radiant effulgence. **Even during the 'Timeless epoch' of  Enlightenment, one's state of Pure Being remains in a state of, now fully Aware, internal radiance manifesting like a crystal does upon being hit by sunlight, only when the secondary circumstances of sentient beings to be trained act as a catalyst for its radiant effulgence.**

As the Dzogchen cycles of Teachings are very profound, aiming at the total Realization of the Nature of Mind in one lifetime into the total dissolution of materiality into its nature of light, **they can only be transmitted and taught by a Teacher which holds an uninterrupted transmission of lineage and has realized in his or her stream of Being the Primordial Awareness of Pure Being** beyond time and space, birth and death. **Dzogchen teachings, therefore, despite being widely available, cannot be applied by simply reading a book.**


## Mind, Pure Being and sentient beings

Having established the characteristics of Mind, let's analyze now the relationship between Mind and sentient beings.

Since all pervasive Mind is infinite in space, there is no finite spot which can be considered its center and yet, at the same time, every point of activity may be called its center. Mind extends in every direction infinitely and its circumference is nonexistent. **This** great all pervasive Mind of Pure Being which is oneself has its center everywhere and its circumference nowhere.

**This great Mind is filled with an infinite number of centers of energy, where each dynamic individual being is such a center for himself or herself, a 'center of living Will' and each one has the whole universe or dimension circling and revolving around him/her.** To symbolize this relationship between Mind and beings some spiritual Teachings employ the symbol of a circle with a dot in the middle.

Some beings are the centers of a tiny dimension, and some have huge dimensions revolving around them. There are centers so expanded and exalted that the human mind cannot grasp, but even the tiniest point of activity is a center in itself and for itself. **The lucid Expanse of Pure Being and sentient beings are integrated beyond any finite conceptual logic.**

The Principle of Mind  also entails that infinite space and all contained therein is occupied by the 'Mind stuff', **an all pervasive Awareness pulsating with life and energy,** in the depths of which there is a timeless calm and on the surface of which are waves, currents and whirlpools pulsating in rhythmic fashion. **Each dynamic individual sentient being is the center and the totality of the infinite Universe revolving around him/her, and yet there are virtually infinite numbers of beings. As far as space extends there is the infinite Principle of Being and an infinite number of sentient beings to fill this vast expanse of Mind.** The individual or personal manifestations of Mind, are centers of 'mentative' energy in the great ocean of universal 'mentative' energy.

Although no example can fit the description of Reality, one possible example could be an ocean, an infinite body of water, where water is 'the totality' and at the same time, 'infinitely individualized' as each totality of water. Another example is the sky or space, in this case an 'aware all pervasive reflective space' at the same time generalized as the totality of all events and meanings and individually reflecting itself as aware individual beings. **All sentient beings are self-reflections of the uncreated all-pervading pure and lucid Expanse of Pure Being which recognizes itself through them.**

## Infinite cognitions within Space-like Timeless Mind

Timeless Mind is a oneness without identity like infinite space but endowed with infinite cognitions, each cognition integrated like space is integrated with space. Each cognition is either an Awakened being or a sentient being depending on whether the cognition recognizes its own timelessness and oneness with all other cognitions (Awakened Awareness of Pure Being) or not (a sentient being lost in infinite conditioned existence).

Each unawakened cognition (sentient being) is individually responsible for finding its own freedom from the suffering of conditioned existence, it cannot awaken another cognition. But all cognitions can affect each other depending on the level of intentions, causes and conditions manifesting and the level of knowledge of the oneness of all cognitions.

All cognitions are individually many and all integrated with each other in timeless oneness. But even though while this infinite and endless drama of 'light and darkness', joy and suffering unfold, the potentiality of the Mind of Pure Being at the heart of all beings whether Awakened or lost in self-grasping, remains self-perfected and unpolluted by both 'light and darkness', joy and sorrow, like a crystal or like the surface of a mirror.

## The will of personality and the spontaneous Will power of Mind in the Hermetic tradition

The Hermetic teachings speak of two kinds of 'will'. **The first one is the will of personality, it is the ego-centered drive or compulsion to act in a certain way and it depends on the intention underlining its actions.** It is also generally known as 'will power 'to accomplish intended actions and is merely a form of intense desire and stubbornness, sometimes it can even be harmful to oneself and others.

It is often used in form of 'authoritative suggestions', assertions and assumption and it can also be responsible for all the phenomena of mental influence, fascinations, suggestions, hypnotism, and 'en-masse' manipulation.

The conditions produced by the application of ego-centered will-power will only hang together as long as the compelling force continues, but when that is exhausted or withdrawn, the elements and situations forced into unnatural combination will at once go back to their proper affinities according to the Law of Cause and Effect and the Law of Vibration. **The circumstances created by ego driven compulsion never have the germ of vitality of Pure Being and are therefore dissipated as soon as the external energy which supports them is withdrawn.** An example of this is all the actions of human beings compelling others under their control, or the use of 'magic' and 'spirit force' or spirit evocation to affect circumstances. **When the compelling force behind is exhausted the karmic force bounces back with an immense power to the originating source.**

The spontaneous Will of power Mind, on the other hand, is the universal energy of Mind, it is the universal energy or the Spirit of Being, the outward manifestation of the 'I AM'. **This Will is that energy power, in both the Universe and in individual sentient beings, which is ever moving, changing its manifestations, flowing, evolving, proceeding, becoming and accomplishing effortlessly.** It contains within itself the potentiality of everything, but it cannot be said to be any of the things it manifests. The Will is clear and colorless like pure, limpid water, **it experiences the color of thoughts, emotions and feelings, but it is never mixed with the latter since it is only the vehicle for the emotion or feeling,** it is its vital energy of Mind so to speak.

**The spontaneous Will of Mind is real power, because it is the potential of infinite manifestation of activities, it is the plastic essence which molds itself into any and all forms, it is the breath of life itself, the 'Holy Spirit'.** It is the essence of all activity which manifests all forms and life, and once it is recognized it may be drawn upon as a source of unending strength and accomplishment. **All beings are 'centers of living Will power' in the great Space of all pervasive Mind.**

Often the mistake is in attributing the creative power to the will of personality or ego-centered will. The correct idea is not to create through ego-effort, but to combine and distribute that which is already in being through recognition, so that what one calls one's creations are only new combinations of already existing energy whether mental, spiritual or physical.

When one feels a sense of mental relation, recognition and identity with the spontaneous Will power of Mind, and allows this inexhaustible energy to flow through one's being, one finds a reservoir of Will power which is inexhaustible and never failing. But if, out of conceit arising from some successful ego-driven action, one begins to think that this power is due to some 'personal strength' or mistakes it with the will of personality, then one may easily become conceited with the pride of personality separating oneself from the source of real power and the universal supply.

## The conscious and the subconscious mind

The Hermetic teachings speak of two aspects of an individual's mind. **The first aspect is the conscious mind or objective mind. It is the mind which knows the objects of the senses and is aware of its own thoughts and emotions.** It is also that aspect of the mind that is able to reason and discriminate. **We can compare the conscious mind to the first seven aspects of consciousness spoken of in the Buddhist 'Mind Only' school.** If we use it with the presence of awareness it becomes the guardian at the door of the subconscious mind, ensuring that only wanted and empowering messages are allowed through.

**The subconscious mind on the other hand is an incredibly powerful program that runs every aspect of our life automatically, organizing and re-organizing without the need for any conscious effort.** It is equivalent to the eighth aspect of consciousness (the ground or storehouse consciousness) of the Buddhist 'Mind Only' school.

In the subconscious mind are stored all our beliefs about reality and all the habitual tendencies which manifests as intuitions, tendencies to feel joy and sorrow and to react in a certain way to any given event; basically all aspects of our waking and dream life. **The subconscious mind cannot distinguish between what is real and what is imagined, it responds automatically through the Law of Cause and Effect and the Law of Vibration with instincts and habits which are manifested into our waking life.**

The subconscious mind does not process negatives, or rejections, and for this reason when we will learn how to use affirmations, statements and creative visualizations we will see how we must always use them in an affirmative sense. **The subconscious represses memories with unresolved negative emotions, the memories get buried, yet the beliefs, feelings and emotions associated with them are able to control our reactions.**
The subconscious works with symbols and associations, and it processes everything in the first person. For example whenever we criticize, judge and project negative thoughts and feelings onto others, **we experience that negativity as our own.**

**It also works with the principle of least effort by following the path of least resistance, like all nature does.** Without a proper and purposeful direction from our conscious mind through the presence of awareness, **it follows the easiest, but sometimes more negative path of our habitual tendencies.**

There is no future or past in the subconscious mind, since it can only process the present time, all stored experiences are processed in the ever present 'now' of our conscious life.

As we have seen the whole of mind can be compared to an iceberg floating in the ocean, where consciousness is the tip of the iceberg, consisting of information and stimuli of which we are aware. **The subconscious is the deep underside of the mind, recording and processing information continuously and connecting the individual to the all-embracing Mind of Pure Being.**

## Mind and consciousness

To summarize, Mind is the source of all phenomena and reality, it is the potentiality of all events, meanings and circumstances and it is beyond all dualistic apprehensions of subjects and objects, time and space.

Mind is at the same time immanent and transcendent of phenomena, **it is an all pervading lucid and reflective Awareness contained in and containing all the phenomena of the Universe and beings**, and it is therefore an immutable, unchanging and non-modifiable state beyond the passing of time and transitions in space, just like the all containing, even, lucid and potentially reflective surface of a mirror. Mind is the source of all aspects of sentient beings consciousness, the source of the conscious and the subconscious mind as we understand it in Western neuro-science and psychology and the source of all physical and non-physical forms.

**Mind is uncreated and uncompounded, it is beyond the Principle of Cause and Effect and therefore it cannot be improved upon or developed by any spiritual or non-spiritual methods, it is and remains an even Principle of all pervading Awareness beyond transition and change to be recognized by the individual.** It is the source of, it pervades, and it is the real nature of all sentient beings. Whether one is a human being, an animal, a ghost, an angel or a demon, one's fundamental Mind of Pure Being does not change and it cannot be polluted by any emotions, thoughts or intentions whether they be positive or negative.

**Consciousness or self-grasping mind, on the other hand, is the offspring of Mind, it is the radiation or effulgence of Mind,** it is like the reflection appearing in a mirror as much as any visible and invisible form. Consciousness is the basis for grasping at an independent self-entity in time and space, it is the basis and the 'machinery' of ego-grasping and ego functioning. Consciousness is synonym with mind, whether conscious, unconscious or subconscious, it operates in dualistic terms in its active phase as the conscious mind, and it is the 'storehouse' of all past experiences in its 'non dual' phase as the subconscious mind. Since it can be worked on and molded at will it can become one's worst enemy or one's best friend in achieving a joyful and fulfilling life (see chapter eight).

**Unlike Mind, consciousness or mind, is within the Principle of Cause and Effect and therefore it can be 'manipulated' and developed in various ways using various methods, it can be improved to an incredible degree or rendered very subtle and 'infinitely stretched out' and in fact there exist so many methods in various spiritual and non-spiritual traditions with this aim.**

Even though through meditation and other similar methods, consciousness can be rendered so peaceful and spacious as to achieve a state of blissful rapture, and so limpid and clear as to develop acute intelligence, infallible memory, clairvoyance and similar powers, **it still is and will always remain the domain of self-grasping, a 'time bound' phenomenon of subject and object**, useful but not the ultimate Truth of Pure Being, not the *'Truth that will set you free'* from illusion-like birth and death.

**On the other hand, a permanent recognition and realization of Reality is accompanied by a spontaneous adornment of inconceivable spiritual virtuous qualities and powers beyond the limits of transition and change.**

## The brain is not the mind

Although science often tells us that consciousness or mind and thoughts are produced by the brain, the Hermetic teachings (and also most spiritual wisdom traditions) affirm that **the brain only functions as a converter or 'transformer' of the mind or consciousness into usable forms like thoughts and emotions.**

The brain is a kind of 'laboratory' of the personal manifestation of mind, and brain building is the development and growth of brain cells and neuro-pathways in any specific region of the brain.

In fact, by developing certain brain cells or neuro-pathways in any specific region of the brain, by using the skillful methods presented in part two of the book, the quality, activity or faculty which uses that specific region for its functioning is greatly increased and rendered more effective. More information about this subject will be given in chapter eight in the 'character building' section.


## Conclusions on the Principle of Mind

**Reality, Mind, Pure Being, The Primordial State or God cannot be described through words, concept and ideas,** therefore it is clear that the underlying message and aim behind all of the different spiritual traditions can only have the function of *'pointing in one direction'*, **that is, toward the individual personal experience, familiarization and total Realization of one's real Nature of Mind, the fundamental Expanse of Pure Being, the true nature of the individual and phenomena, depending on the culture, language, intellectual and spiritual acumen and inclination of the different sentient beings involved,** always bearing in mind that no formula, explanation nor example will ever be able to describe every side of Reality.


*"Do not investigate the root of things,*
*investigate the root of Mind!*
*Once the Mind's root has been found,*
*you'll know one thing, yet all is thereby freed.*
*But if the root of Mind you fail to find,*
*you will know everything but nothing understand"*

*Padmasambhava - The lotus born Buddha*

# Chapter 2

# The Principle of Cause and Effect

*"Every Cause has its Effect; every Effect has its Cause; everything happens according to Law; chance is but a name for the  Law  not recognized; there are many planes of causation, but nothing escapes the Law."*

*The Kybalion*

## Law, not fate is the axiom of the Hermetic tradition

In general one can identify two kinds of beliefs in modern human society, either that one's  life is ruled or guided by an external supreme and all-knowing being which has been called God, able to intervene and shape the affairs of the world or that life is just chance, fate, good or bad luck and that the universe is in a state of chaos or chaotic chance. **Most people hold either one of these views regarding Reality or a confused mixture of both.**

According to the Kybalion and, as we will see later, most western and eastern philosophical and spiritual traditions, both of these beliefs are wrong views since they are not based on the Laws governing Reality and can be considered either 'eternalistic' or 'nihilistic'.

**In fact everything manifested in the Universe and in each individual's life, happens according  to unchanging Laws, of which the Law of Cause end Effect is one of the most important, because not only it rules all planes of Reality but it is the fundamental Law for the  arising  of  different  kinds  of phenomena in one's perception.**

In the Bible, for example, the Law of Cause and Effect is revealed in the statement: **'As you sow, you shall reap' (Galatians 6:7)** where we are introduced to the truth that what one wishes for others or does to others sooner or later one will have to experience in one's own life.

In fact nothing ever 'merely happens', and there is no such thing as chance, in fact a careful examination will show that **what we call chance is merely a common  expression regarding causes that we cannot perceive or  that we cannot understand.**

If you toss a coin in the air you might get a 'heads' or 'tails', but even this single toss comes under the Law of Cause and Effect, because if one were able to examine into the preceding causes, one would clearly see that, given exactly the same causes and conditions and at the same time and place of the event, it would have been impossible for the coin to fall down other than the way it did.

**Therefore, given the same relative circumstances of time and place to mature or activate such primary causes, the same result always follows.** Nothing ever 'happens' by chance but there is always a 'cause', or rather a chain of causes and conditions behind it. **According to this Principle, what we call good luck or bad luck is really the energetic 'pushes and pulls' of primary causes and the circumstantial energy of the time and the place (the Law of Vibration) combined, which give rise to that specific 'lucky' or 'unlucky' event we call chance.**

No event produces another event, but is merely a preceding link in the great orderly chain of events flowing from the creative energy of Pure Being or Mind Principle. There is continuity between all events and also a relation existing between everything that has gone before, and everything that follows. Every thought we think, everything we say and every act we perform, has its direct and indirect consequence which fits into the great chain of Cause and Effect.

**There is usually a time gap between the cause and the following effect which always depends on many secondary conditions in order to manifest.** Sometimes secondary conditions favor the activation of more negative causes to manifest and sometimes they favor more positive causes, but sooner or later all causes will manifest as effects and shape one's life circumstances (see also the chapter 'understanding astrology, and the meaning of luck and fortune').

In general terms, we can never set any cause in motion without calling forth those effects which it already contains in embryo and which will again become causes in their turn, thus producing a series of causes and effects which must continue to flow on '*ad infinitum*' until we bring into operation a cause of an opposite character to the one which originated it or we employ a specific method of counteraction (a spiritual or psychological practice of some kind). **Whenever a primary cause has been planted, just like a seed in a field, if it doesn't meet any hindrances, it is definite that it will bring the result, whatever it is.**

Just like a perfect seed surrounded by the right secondary circumstances will take time to ripe, causes take time to manifest as visible effects. But if the primary cause meets a hindrance, or it is counteracted by a primary cause of an opposite nature then it is possible that it won't bring a full result, that one won't have to experience the effect. A clear example of this is the planting of a seed in a fertile ground, which, even though it has the ability to grow, there is always the chance to disturb the conditions that cause the seed to produce the plant, for example by taking the seed out or to burn it, or by pouring hot water over it etc.

Not only that, but there are various planes of Cause and Effect, the higher planes of mind and energy dominating the lower planes of matter, and, as we will see later, we can work with this in order to set new causes in motion and alter circumstances, **still nothing ever entirely escapes the Law of Cause and Effect. One must obey the causation of the higher planes, and rule the one on the lower planes.**

Another important fact in understanding causation is that external actions are not the only causative power, but there is another aspect of the law of causation, namely, that of pure intended-thought, a power which is able to start a new sequence of causation not related to any past actions.

We should be aware also that the further the causation is from the primary source of Pure Being, the more it is bound by impelling conditions, and the nearer to the primary source, the freer it is. This will become clearer in the eighth chapter where we learn how to employ this principle in order to alter one's circumstances.

Mind as pure potentiality is beyond time, space and beyond any Laws, but its manifestation is always governed by unchanging Laws.


## The Law of Cause and Effect or Karma in the Buddhist tradition

*"Then the Buddha explained the Karma Sutra: "Destiny is the aggregate karmic effects from past life. Past Karma determined your present destiny. Present Karmas are to mould your next life. Learn the law of Karma expounded as follows".*

*The Golden Precepts by Shakyamuni Buddha*

We can find the Law of Cause and Effect in many spiritual traditions, and many people nowadays are accustomed to the word 'Karma' which in fact means 'action'.

The Principle of Karma is well explained in the Hindu and especially in the Buddhist tradition where the Law of Karma is a central topic as the Buddha explained it in many major teachings called 'Sutras'.

**The Buddha explained that all the feelings of happiness, unhappiness, and neutral feelings (for example boredom) accompany every single moment of each being's existence and are due to not knowing the real condition of Reality and the subsequent formation of Karma,** the setting in motion of the endless chain of Cause and Effect through the twelve interdependent links of karmic formation.

In Buddhism, Karma is not only the physical action, but also the verbal action **and especially the mental impulse or urge to act through intention oriented thoughts** which brings one in the direction of a particular experience. **In a nutshell Karma in**

Buddhism is motivation and what is motivated. That's why one can accumulate good and bad Karma just by wishing an outcome with a strong motivation.

The action itself is a positive or a negative karmic force, which sometimes is called merit or non-virtue, which, when completed, carries its karmic effect, which continues within one's mental continuum as a  karmic tendency or constant habits to repeat the action though body, speech and mind.

**For a complete karmic cause to be set in motion we always need four factors: the basis of the action or the object at which the action is aimed, the intention to act based on a motivation which can be positive, negative or neutral, the action itself needs to be carried out directly or indirectly, and afterward we need to be satisfied or at least feel no regret.**

If one of these  four factors is not present the karmic consequence will be less heavy but that doesn't mean that there will be no results,  **in this later case we speak of a 'karmic impediment' which will contribute to the maturation of other karmic primary causes similar in nature.**

There can be physical and verbal actions, but these usually start with mental urges, or mental Karmas. The urge to do something comes before the actual action and it is often accompanied by its own compelling emotion.


## The ripening of different Karmas

There are three general rules regarding the ripening of Karma.

- **The first is the certainty of the result**, which means that unless it meets a hindrance or one purifies a negative action or neutralize it with a positive action of the same nature and weight, the result will never disappear until the right circumstances for its ripening present themselves. **Connected to this is the fact that the passing of time does not wear off a karmic cause.** But even though infinite Karma has been created, there is always the chance to change it and to not experience its result by completely purifying it or counteracting it with a primary cause of an opposite nature, which is like destroying the ability of the seed to grow.

- **The second rule of ripening is the increase of result** which means that from a small action very large results can follow.
- The third is that **if one has not committed a certain action, one will not experience its results** even if the secondary circumstances present themselves, although one would still experience the effect of planned actions which one didn't actually commit in person, but told someone else to do, like for example paying someone to kill someone etc.

In Buddhism it is explained that Karma ripens as an effect in four different ways:

- The first is **the effect of maturation**, the experience of one's birth aggregates, like the type of body and mind or intelligence one has, and the particular dimension in which one has been reborn. For example in the phenomenal plane of sensuous desire, (see chapter four on the different planes of existence), a mind dominated by anger is the cause for rebirth in the dimension of the various hells, predominant and persistent accumulation of greed and attachment causes one to be born as a starving spirit, accumulation of persistent and dense states of very dimmed awareness or confusion of mind without the ability of discernment of what to accept and what to reject causes the birth as one type of animal. Humans are caused by a more or less equal mix of different emotions and the accumulation of virtuous intentions and actions (although in the human realm one can also notice all the different degrees of suffering and joy depending on the predominant emotion), heavenly 'god like' beings are caused by predominant pride and a great store of accumulated virtuous intentions and actions.

- The second is **the effect in agreement with the cause or of compatibility,** which is the urge or compulsion in every moment to do or say something similar to what we did before and experience its effects.
- The third is called **the cumulative effect** which can be related to the environment in which we are born and in that rebirth, all the various feelings of happiness and unhappiness we experience. **The cumulative effect is also connected to the collective karma of all sentient beings inhabiting and shaping a certain environment** and dimension (see chapter four).
- The fourth is **the cumulative effect of ripening,** or the tendency  to experience a situation similar to what we did, with the same situations  happening back to us over and over, (we kill once and we are killed sequentially many times), one cause can ripen into many effects.

There is also the differentiation between **'throwing and completing Karma'.** The former being the causes that have the potentiality to 'throw' us into the next birth, and the latter being the ones responsible for shaping our rebirth, for example we can be reborn as dog due to the throwing karmic causes, but then, depending on the completing causes, we could be either a stray dog in constant search for food or a pet in some rich household.

This is because, certain causes produce precise effects, for example actions of generosity through one's physical, verbal and mental actions produce wealth and enjoyments, the cause of not killing but saving other's lives produces a long life and freedom from illness, the cause of saying the truth and not lying produces the effect that others listen to what we have to say and believe in us and so on (see chapter eight:  'the most important points of causation').

**In a nutshell, the karmic result of any action is always based on the intention or motivation behind it, what seems to be a positive action can actually have a negative effect if the motivation behind is not entirely positive. One could say that what we are and perceive in each moment is the sum of all one's**

intentions and motivations accumulated in this life and in infinite past lives.

## Different degrees of ripening

The karmic consequence of one's actions can ripen into something strong or into something light and this depends on many factors.

- **The first factor is the nature of the action involved.** This is in terms of the suffering or happiness that it causes the object of one's action.
- **The second is the strength of the emotion**, negative or positive, that accompanies the action. Hurting someone with really strong hatred is much worse than hurting them with just a little bit of anger.
- **The third is the distorted, compelling drive, based on the wrong view,** in other words, whether or not we believe that doing a certain action is perfectly all right and anybody who thinks the opposite is wrong or stupid.
- **The fourth is the basis at which the action is aimed.** This varies according to the amount of benefit we or others have received from that being in the past and according to the good qualities of the being involved.
- **The fifth is the frequency or habits to do such action**, for example if we have done a certain action many times in the past it is heavier than just doing it once.
- **The sixth is the number of people involved in committing the action**, committing actions in groups is heavier than committing them alone, the power of emotions involved add up with the number of people involved.
- **The seventh is the power of regret and the presence or absence of opposing forces.** For example, if we do something negative, whether or not we counterbalance it with a lot of positive actions or feel regret and decide not to repeat the action. A negative action is very heavy if we

don't regard it as a mistake. What opposes that is admitting that it was a mistake even if we didn't think there was anything wrong with it when we did it. If we admit that it was a mistake afterwards it will start to purify the consequences or at least make them less heavy.

- **Last but not least is the power of rejoicing in the positive or negative actions and attitudes of others**. If we rejoice in the positive actions of others, we build up positive karmic force and if we rejoice in the destructive or negative actions of others, we build up a negative karmic force and both of these attitudes will have an effect on one's life.

## The karmic flood

The most common question in general people have about Cause and Effect is why some sentient beings seem to commit all sorts of negative actions and live a seemingly wealthy and healthy life and some others which dedicate themselves to many virtuous actions, especially spiritual in kind, seem to suffer from all sorts of obstacles.

The answer to this has many aspects: first Karma, Cause and Effect is not some kind of 'justice maker' which sits there and decides who is to get what kind of specific punishment for this or that action; second, **causes ripen and manifest into specific effects only when the secondary circumstances are conducive for this to happen regardless of the passing of time, whether it will be a minute or a million years**; and third, and most important, Karma sometimes tends to manifest a kind of 'karmic flood' for some beings which indulge in extremely positive or negative intending actions.

**This manifests in a way in which one tends to 'use up' all positive or negative store of primary causes while engaging in an opposite lifestyle to the causes that are manifesting.** In other words, someone committing a great deal of negative deeds might experience a great deal of positive circumstances and therefore 'use up' all meritorious causes with the consequence of  ending up in the most distressful life circumstances and environment for a very long time and many lifetimes to come.

On the contrary, someone which is engaging in skillful and virtuous activities, and especially of a spiritual kind, might experience all sorts of mildly negative circumstances in order to consume all residual negative karmas until the total consummation of all negative Karma after which he or she would only pass from one joyful event to the next until total liberation and Awakening beyond time and beyond Cause and Effect. This is why one should never envy or compare oneself with pride to other beings, since nobody knows what is going to happen next, which causes one has planted or are about to ripen.

**In most cases, and for most sentient beings, though, Causes and Effects manifest in a more mixed kind of fashion, almost 'haphazardly' because of their depending on specific secondary circumstances for their ripening which are constantly changing.**


## Karma and compassion for suffering

The knowledge that all events and circumstances unfold due to precise causes and conditions should not make one become judgmental and cold hearted toward the suffering of living beings.
**On the contrary, knowing how difficult it is to become aware of one's nature of Pure Being and to be able to change the conditioning of primary causation should inspire oneself to develop unconditioned love and compassion toward oneself and others.**

One should also avoid feeling proud, arrogant and complacent when wealth, good health and fortune manifest because of past virtuous actions as nobody knows what primary causes one has planted during infinite lifetimes and which one is going to manifest next, the Laws of Rhythm and Ciclicity and the effect of compensation are always at work with unerring precision (see chapter five and six).

By developing a sense of love and compassion for all beings, one is able to plant more and more primary causes which will definitely result in more joyful events to manifest in one's field of perception.


## Understanding astrology and the meaning of luck and fortune

**As stated at the beginning of this chapter, what generally is regarded as good or bad luck is really the energetic 'pushes and pulls' of primary causes activated by the  circumstantial energy of the time and place combined with the Law of Vibration which all combined give rise to that specific 'lucky' or  'unlucky' event to manifest in one's field of perception.**

We can therefore understand that the position of planets and constellations is part of what we call the 'circumstantial energy of the time and place' which can become part of the secondary circumstances for the activation and unfolding of primary causes which otherwise would not manifest. Also what we call planets and stars is only what our limited senses can perceive.

**We perceive only what we have the causes to perceive as an individual (and shared) perception.** Imagine a small ant walking very fast on your chest on a hot summer day, what kind of perception would it have of you? Maybe according to its sense perception you are an enormous unknown 'X' hanging somewhere in space in its outer dimension. **What we perceive as phenomenal reality with our senses is only a limited distorted portion of what is.**

For example if one has planted many causes of wealth by being selflessly generous, the effect will manifest when certain energies in the seemingly 'outside' world (one's perception) act as secondary conditions for those specific primary causes to be activated and manifest.

This is because the Law of Correspondence and the Law of Vibration work interdependently and in synergy with the Law of Cause and Effect.

In a nutshell, **astrology is the knowledge of what is circumstantial in time and space in a particular dimension, it does not predict what will be, but can help in activating and making manifest what is potential** because of specific primary causes. Fortune is the positive potential of virtuous primary causes manifesting in time and space as an event due to secondary favorable circumstances, misfortune and bad luck is its opposite.

*"The whole world is cause and effect; excluding this, there is no sentient being. From factors (which are) only empty, empty factors originate".*

*The Stanzas of the Heart of Interdependent Origination*

*Nāgārjuna (150–250 CE)*

*"I am the owner of my karma. I inherit my karma. I am born of my karma. I am related to my karma. I live supported by my karma. Whatever karma I create, whether good or evil, that I shall inherit".*

*Upajjhatthana Sutra -The Buddha*

*"Deep and quiet, simple, clear, unformed.*
*A truth that is like nectar I have found.*
*Whoever I explain it, no one will understand.*
*So, in the jungle, silent, I remain".*

*The Buddha's Awakening*

# Chapter 3

# The Principle of Vibration or Sound

*"Mind (as well as metals and elements) may be transmuted from state to state; degree to degree; condition to condition; pole to pole; vibration to vibration."*

*The Kybalion*

**The Principle of Vibration tells us that everything, from the totality of the Mind of Pure Being, to the heart of each sentient being and down to the grossest form of matter, all is in motion and everything vibrates.** The higher the vibration, the higher the position in the scale or the closer it is to the primal cause of Pure Being.

Here a paradox is introduced because in the first chapter of the Kybalion it is stated that the center of Mind is a place of rest on the surface of which there are waves, currents and whirlpools and centers of energy. **But as the Law of Polarity tells us, opposites are identical in nature, but different in degree, extremes meet, all truths are half-truths, and all paradoxes are reconciled.**

**The Expanse of Pure Being vibrates at such an infinite rate of intensity and rapidity that it is practically at rest, just as a rapidly moving wheel seems to be motionless**. But at the other end of the scale, there are gross forms of matter whose vibrations are so low as to seem at rest too.

On a physical scale, the Universe, when resolved into the infinity of nothingness at the end of a cosmic cycle (see chapter six), is practically motionless, the Principle of Vibration being in a condition of absolute rest, and yet, this absolute rest is analogous to motion of such a high degree of vibration as to be practically motionless and at rest at the same time. **In this condition the two poles of vibration have been resolved into** one, the extremes have merged and absolute motion and absolute rest are seen to be identical.

In a nutshell, the differences between the various manifestations of the play of Reality on all dimensional planes are due entirely to the different degrees and modes of vibration.


## Vibration and Sound

In the first chapter we have discovered that spreading throughout limitless space there is a universal medium, an ocean of Mind power, **now we come to understand that through this universal medium of Mind is possible to convey and receive information by means of vibrations which can be set into motion by the power of sound.**

In the physical world of matter, by instance, science states that energy waves travel through the ether until they come in contact with matter capable of taking up their vibrations. **The Hermetic teachings of the Kybalion speak of the ether as a fine form of matter, filling all space, even between the atoms, as well as between the worlds.**

In the view of this, all objects in our universe emit, reflect, and absorb electromagnetic waves in their own distinctive ways, for example thermal radiation propagates without the presence of matter through the vacuum of space as a direct result of the random movements of atoms and molecules in matter. Since these atoms and molecules are composed of charged particles (protons and electrons), their movement results in the emission of electromagnetic radiation, which carries energy away from the surface.

Let's take as an example the emission of light by the sun. In this case the 'original' light and heat of the sun does not travel to the earth to be then experienced by the latter, but, on the contrary, the original solar heat and light sets up the waves in the ether, which travel along until the earth is reached, and, when meeting with the proper material, they are reproduced or 'transformed' into heat and light vibrations 'similar' to those of the original impulse so that people on  earth can feel the heat and see the light.

**Therefore light is simply a form of energy and the only 'real light' is the sensation caused in the mind by the motion of energy waves**. Moreover, when the intensity of vibrations of light waves increases, light changes its color, each change in color being caused by shorter and more rapid vibrations, so that although we speak of the rose as being red, the grass as being green, or the sky as being blue, we know that the colors exist only in our minds and are caused by the sensations experienced by us as the result of the vibrations of light waves.

Another example is the waves in water, where even though it seems that a series of waves apparently travel toward the shore, in real sense the motion is passed on and another wave is formed, then another, and another, until there is the seeming motion of waves in water. **In reality the waves don't travel, they merely communicate their motion to the water particles next to them and a continuous moving effort is exhibited.** Electricity and magnetism are reproduced in the same way, in fact, **all waves are alike in this respect, all of them communicate vibrations, which move on in a 'wave like' motion though the ether.**

Just so, vibration  activity in the form  of sound, thought, emotion, reason, will or desire, or any other mental condition for that matter, arising in one's mind and the minds of infinite beings, 'pass on' in the all-pervading great ocean of Mind, to  produce waves or currents of energy, which travel or move on until they reach the mind of other beings *'tuned in'* to the same vibration (or frequency), in which they tend to reproduce by induction the original vibrations or mental  states in a *'like attracts like'* fashion.

**As we will see in chapter eight, by mastering the Principle of Vibration and the Principle of Polarity, one may polarize one's mind to any degree (or frequency) one wishes, thus gaining control over one's mental states, thoughts and feelings, producing 'thoughts and emotional vibrations' at will.**

## The Principle of Vibration (or Sound) in the Christian tradition

The Principle of Vibration can be found in different spiritual traditions, and in the Bible we find a citation as in the following verses: *"In the beginning was the Word, and the Word was with God, and the Word was God. John 1:1"*.

Here 'Word' obviously stands for vibration and sound, and in this case sound is the essence of God itself, or we could say the energy of Pure Being (God) in the general and individualized aspects, able to start a sequence of manifestation, whether in the macrocosmic or in the microcosmic dimensions of phenomena.

## The Principle of Vibration (or Sound) in Buddhist Tantra

In the tradition of Tantric Buddhism we find the Principle of Vibration expressed in the inner practices of transformation where one imagines and develops a 'Mandala', or a pure vision of the dimension of a particular Deity or Enlightened Being, which is a *'facsimile'* of the 'real' dimension of that Deity (the spontaneous effulgent radiance of Reality), in order to transform one's limited dualistic vision of reality into the total vision of Enlightenment and realize the qualities of Enlightened Wisdom through that particular Deity.

**The Buddhist Tantric Deities are symbols and 'personification' of 'Timeless Awakened Mind' and not the deities or god-like living beings described in the next chapter, as those beings, although considered as deities are still bound by ignorance of the true nature of Reality.**

While in the Dzogchen path to self-realization (see chapter one on the Principle of Mind) one recognizes directly one's nature of Pure Being and integrates all dualistic experiences in that state **(in other words one identifies oneself with the lucid mirror-like Expanse of Mind and experiences one's own reflections as self-**

**appearances),** in the Buddhist higher path of Tantric transformation, one uses precise symbols in the form of Deities (equivalent to the mirror's pure reflections) to discover and abide in the nature of the potentiality of Pure Being which is reflecting (equivalent to the mirror's lucid surface potentiality).

Moreover, in Buddhist Tantric transformation one also uses sounds in the form of different Sanskrit syllable (mantras) which represent the energy of that particular Deity in order to enhance the feeling and the reality of the creative visualization.

**The Tantric practitioner employs 'mantras', or strings of Sanskrit syllables which are the natural vibration or energy of Pure Being manifested by that particular Deity,** in order to integrate or transform one's limited 'periscopic' vision into the total vision of Reality itself.

Ultimately the Deity serves as a symbol which allows the practitioner to integrate one's three aspects of body, speech and dualistic mind into the total and non-dual nature of Enlightened Wisdom, the Nature of Mind beyond the dualistic distinctions of one and many. On a more relative level, by using Tantric transformation and specific 'mantras' one is also capable of actualizing specific relative actions or qualities for the benefit of oneself and others. For example the 'development' of specific qualities like healing, intelligence, purification of negative Karma, increasing wealth and prosperity, magnetizing beings , eliminating negative obstacles through fierce activities and protecting the mind from negative influences and destructive emotions.

**These actions or qualities, however, are not developed anew with the practice, but simply revealed through the practice as inherent qualities of Mind's Nature.** These actions are considered 'magical' actions as they manipulate one's perception of the world at will, but in order to be able to actualize them one needs to have developed a firm realization of oneself as a Deity, a symbol of the power intrinsic to Pure Being. **In a nutshell, to act like a Deity one needs to really feel oneself as a Deity.** Since reality evolves from all pervading Awareness into personal perception, one uses the symbol of the Deity as a *'magnifying glass'* in order to use the power intrinsic to Pure Being and set oneself free from the bonds of ordinary causality as a temporary accomplishment, and finally realize the ultimate accomplishment of Awakening into the state of the Deity as the Expanse of Pure Being itself.

**The 'shared public reality' manifested into one's perception by the workings of ordinary Karma, Cause and Effect, is to the Tantric Practitioner an illusory reality, just as true and just as false as the reality he or she can evoke from the potentiality of Pure Being.** It must be noted that, in general, certain mantras associated to the primordial natural vibration or sound of the Deity, have also an independent power outside the Tantric transformation framework, and can be used and directed by a practitioner who has the capacity to do so.

The Buddhist Tantric system or vehicle leading to Enlightenment is sometimes also called, the 'resultant vehicle' (as opposed to the 'causal vehicle' of the Sutra system) because the path is no longer based on establishing the cause, **but by identifying oneself directly with the fruition (the effect),** the fundamentally pure Nature of Mind and its qualities and activities, through the use of symbols of Enlightened Deities.

Buddhist Tantric transformation, despite being widely applied nowadays in certain contexts, is not as easy as it seems. **This is because of the natural tendency of dualistic mind to grasp at forms and sounds in dualistic terms of a separate subject and object.**

**By considering these Deities, which are visionary manifestations of the pure effulgent radiance of the potentiality of Pure Being beyond space and time, as 'self-existent' beings separate from each other and from oneself, instead of individual symbols of the Wisdom of Enlightenment, and by considering their relative activities in terms of subject and object, one is in danger of reinforcing one's mind dualistic tendencies instead of transforming and dissolving them.**

# Chapter 4

# The Principle of Correspondence

*"As above, so below; as below, so above."*

*The Kybalion*

**The Principle of Correspondence embodies the truth that there is always a correspondence, harmony and agreement between the Laws and phenomena of the various dimensions of existence.** This Principle is of universal application and manifestation on the various planes of the material, mental, and spiritual reality.

Each plane of life has its corresponding manifestations, therefore by studying the physical world one will understand the metaphysical and vice versa.

**In the previous chapter we have seen that everything, from the totality of Mind, which is an Expanse of Pure Being, to the heart of each living being and down to the grossest form of matter, all is in motion and everything vibrates.** We have also seen that the higher the vibration, the higher the position in the scale or the closer it is to the source of Timeless Pure Being.

The degree of the frequency of vibrations constitutes the degree of measurement on the scale of different dimensions of phenomenal reality also called 'planes of existence'.

**The higher the degree of the rate of vibration, the higher the plane and the higher the manifestation of the life principle occupying that dimensional plane.**

These 'planes of existence' are manifestations of the play of Reality and are inhabited by beings which haven't yet realized the nature of Timeless Pure Being, immanent and transcendent Mind.

## The three great dimensions of existence in the Hermetic tradition

The Hermetic tradition speaks of three different planes or dimensions of Reality:

I.   The great physical planes.
II.  The great mental planes.
III. The great spiritual planes.

**Each of these planes is divided into seven sub-divisions according to their rates of vibration and the Law of Cause and Effect.**

The Hermetic teachings regards matter as a form of energy, that is, energy at a low rate of vibration of a certain kind, therefore the **seven physical planes** include three planes of physical matter and three of energy which ranges from the physical energy (heat, light, magnetism, electricity, and gravity or attraction) to the more spiritual energy used by spiritually developed beings and which may be considered 'divine or miraculous power'. These seven physical planes are separated by the plane of ethereal substance which is what science calls 'ether',  a substance of extreme elasticity, pervading all universal space, and acting as a medium for the transmission of waves of physical energy (such as  light,  heat, electricity, radio waves etc) and spiritual energy (the phenomena of 'mentation', mind power etc). This ethereal substance also forms a connecting link between the plane of matter and energy.

The **seven mental planes** comprise minerals, plants, animals and human beings in ascending order according to the Law of Cause and Effect, the Law of Vibration and the degree of mental development expressed by each of them. **Since the first Principle of Mind states that 'All is Mind', the Hermetic teachings consider minerals and plants as expressing a very rudimentary form of 'mindness' or 'mentation'.**

The **seven spiritual planes** include 'god like' beings possessing life, mind, capacities  and forms so exalted compared to the human beings of this era that our mind cannot even conceive. **The life and bodies of these beings are 'clothed in pure energy' vibrating at a very high rate due to such positive spiritual primary causes.**

But even the highest of these advanced 'god like' beings exist merely as a 'reflection' of the play and effulgence of Mind, and are subject to Laws as much as human beings or animals on earth. **These 'god like' beings are still mortal and therefore doomed to endless rebirth until the total realization of Reality.**

## The three worlds or planes of existence in Buddhism

Buddhist cosmology shares many similarities with Hindu **cosmology in terms of cycles of time and type of beings inhabiting the planes of existence, although the names and details can vary in each tradition,** therefore in this chapter I will only describe the Buddhist cosmology.

Buddhist cosmology can be divided into three related branches: spatial cosmology, which describes the arrangement of the various dimensions in a vertical pattern and is related to the beings inhabiting a specific universe; horizontal cosmology which describes how these different dimensions are grouped in the Universe, and temporal cosmology, which describes how the various universes come into existence, remain and how they pass away.

In spatial cosmology we find an explanation of three planes of existence in ascending order which are the dimensions of different types of beings according to the Law of Cause and Effect and the Law of Vibration. **What causes a specific dimension and Universe to manifest is the collective Karma, or the sum of all intending thoughts and emotions and actions of all the beings inhabiting that specific dimension.**

The three worlds are:

    I.   The world of sensuous desire (kāmaloka)
    II.  The world of 'fine matter' (rūpaloka)

III.    The formless world (arūpaloka)

The **world of desire** (kāmaloka) comprises eleven dimensions in ascending order which ranges from hell beings to starving wondering spirits, animals, humans and six types of heavenly 'god like' beings. The beings born in the world of desire are dominated by attachment to the five sense pleasures and the causes to be reborn in each one of them are virtuous or non-virtuous actions committed by body or speech motivated by negative, positive or neutral thoughts- intentions.

**As we have already seen in chapter two, five types of predominant emotions can become the cause for rebirth as a different type of being in the realm of sensuous desire and these emotions also shape the 'manifested environment' experienced by the consciousness  of that specific being.**

A mind dominated by anger is the cause for rebirth in the dimension of the various hells, predominant greed and attachment causes one to be reborn as a starving spirit, a continuous and dense state of dullness and fogginess and confusion, and a very dimmed awareness without the ability of discernment of what to accept and what to reject causes to be born as a type of animal. Humans are caused by a mix of different emotions and the accumulation of virtuous intentions and actions (**although in the human realm one can also notice all the different degrees of suffering and joy depending on the predominant emotion**), heavenly 'god-like' beings are caused by predominant pride and a great store of accumulated virtuous intentions and actions.

**The world of 'fine matter'** (rūpaloka) comprises seventeen different dimensional planes inhabited by 'deities' possessing extremely refined bodies composed of pure light energy which is invisible to the inhabitants of the worlds of desire. **The causes to be reborn in one of these seventeen world dimensions are the attainments of some level of one pointed-concentration or meditation, having developed the clarity of discernment, and at the same time having temporarily suppressed the main emotions of greed, attachment, hatred and ill-will.**

The **formless world** (arūpaloka) is formed by four different dimensional planes of 'just consciousness' inhabited by beings without shape or location. The causes to be reborn as one of these formless beings are the meditative absorptions into one of the four different levels of thoughtless trance, transcendental type of meditation, meditating on one's consciousness as infinitely pervasive or meditating on infinite space and infinite nothingness.

**As discussed in the Hermetic teachings, also in Buddhism and Hinduism, all of these different types of 'dimensional planes' or 'realms' of existence into which beings can be reborn are considered not beyond the cycle of infinite rebirth and therefore bound by impermanence and suffering. The beings born therein have not yet realized the non-dual Timeless Wisdom potentiality of Mind beyond time and space, subject and object.**

## The Principle of Correspondence and modern science

The Principle of Correspondence can also be found in modern science, for example we could observe how there is absolute correspondence between the macrocosm and the microcosm within physical reality.

What happens on the smallest scale happens on an infinite scale, the same principles and laws apply to both. Nowadays new interesting scientific theories about the universe are formulated, one of them asserts that 84 % of the universe is actually made up of 'invisible matter', and that the universe is expanding at a faster and faster rate like a water bubble, due to what is called 'invisible energy' which makes up 68.3% of its total mass-energy.

Another interesting scientific theory is that there are possibly infinite number of 'bubble like' universes, each one being in a different phase of birth, duration and dissolution (this later theory being in complete agreement with Buddhist cosmology).

# Chapter 5

# The Principle of Polarity (or Opposites)

*"Everything is dual, everything has poles, everything has its pair of opposites; like and unlike are the same, opposites are identical in nature, but different in degree; extremes meet; all truths are but half-truths; all paradoxes may be reconciled."*

*The Kybalion*

**The Principle of Polarity or Law of Opposites states that the play of Reality manifests always two sides, or two poles and the difference between these two seemingly diametrically opposed poles is merely a matter of degree.**

This principle implies that thesis and anti-thesis are identical in nature, but different in degree, that every truth is half-false and everything 'is and isn't', at the same time. This Principle is the 'universal principle of reconciliation of opposites' because in the union of the two poles, or pair of opposites, there is to be found the 'thing-in-itself'.

According to the Law of Opposites, everything attains completion by manifesting itself in the opposite direction to that from which it started. **For example the spiritual and the physical planes are in reality the different poles of the same thing: the play of the Expanse of Pure Being.**

Since all is in motion, and all motion is the appearance of energy at another point, wherever the new form reappears, the manifested energy is still the same but at a different degree of vibration. **Even the expanse of Mind and its manifestations are opposite poles of the same nature varying only in degree.**

On the physical plane we have the example of heat and cold being of the same nature in varying degree of temperature, where the lower end of the scale is called 'cold' and the higher is called 'heat' with many degrees between these two. Again, one particular thing may be both good and bad at the same time, that is, good for some purpose and bad for others. The same with directions, if one starts traveling north at some point one will find himself traveling south and vice versa. And so it is with light and dark, inside and outside, the scale of colors, the notes of the musical scale, **all opposites share the same nature in varying degrees.**

The same principle applies to the mental and emotional planes. Love and hate are generally regarded as being diametrically opposed emotions to each other, entirely different, irreconcilable, but in fact there is no such thing as 'absolute love' or 'absolute hate', being merely terms applied to the two poles of the same thing, an emotional vibration. **There is no absolute standard and all is a matter of degree.**

By working with this principle one is able to 'transform' or 'polarize' into any desired state, remembering that the positive pole always overcomes the negative pole, due to the former being of a higher vibration (see chapter three) and the tendency of nature to go in the direction of the dominant activity of the positive pole. **The change is not in the nature of a transmutation of one thing into another thing entirely different, but is merely a change of degree in the same scale of vibration.**

Things which belong to different classes cannot be transmuted into each other, but things belonging to the same class may be changed, by changing their polarity. Likewise emotions of different scales cannot be transmuted into one another, because they must belong to the same scale. Love can never become courage or north or south, or hot or cold, but it may, and evidence shows that often does, turn into hate.

Likewise strong hate may be transformed into love, by changing its polarity; fear may be transformed into courage, hot may be rendered cold and so on, always between things of the same kind but of different degree. The transmutation of seemingly solid elements at will generally called 'Alchemy' is also based on the Principle of Polarity and the Principle of Vibration.

# The Principles of Polarity and Gender in the Bible book of Genesis

*"You will not certainly die" the serpent said to the woman. "For God knows that when you eat from it your eyes will be opened, and you will be like God, knowing good and evil."*

*Genesis 3:4-6 (NIV)*

**The Bible is an Hermetic book of symbols, where the inner and secret meaning is always hidden within symbols sometimes difficult to unravel.** In the above passage, for example, we find a few interesting symbols like the serpent, which by changing its skin and taking on a new physical appearance, symbolizes the force of the sphere of material existence in contrast with the purely spiritual existence of light of the heavens.

The woman is a symbol representing the moving and active aspect and energy function of Mind (and not a female sentient being) according to the Principle of mental Gender which will be discussed in chapter seven. Lastly the Principle of Polarity is introduced with the knowledge of good and evil. **Since the potentiality of Pure Being, a mirror-like all-pervading Awareness of Pure potential is in constant spontaneous manifestation, within the total freedom and majesty of this play of effulgence lays the intrinsic opportunity to stray into the confusion of duality of opposites without recognizing their illusory nature.**

Within and by Timeless Mind, the all-pervading mirror-like Awareness of Pure Being, an array of illusory forms are self-manifested as a spontaneous play, and given the free opportunity to either self-recognition as self-manifestation beyond all opposites (including good and bad), and therefore the possibility to freely partake of  this infinite play of creation without the illusory division of subject and object, or, otherwise, a non-recognition and the subsequent limitation into a dimmed awareness or consciousness and the forming of tightly grasped dualistic concepts of opposite values.

**God, being simply the potentiality of Pure Being, a mirror-like all-pervading Awareness potentiality is free to the extent of letting itself 'forgetting' into the non-recognition its own self-manifestation.**


## The Principle of Polarity in Buddhism

In Mahayana Buddhism, in one of the key texts of the Buddhist Canon, called the '*Prajna Paramita Hridaya*' Sutra, (which literally means 'The Heart of the Perfection of Transcendent Wisdom') commonly known as the 'Heart Sutra' we find one of the most important statement regarding Reality, **a paradox in which the Principle of Polarity or Opposites is transcended in the experience of Perfection of Wisdom, the  non-dual Reality of Pure Being.** From the Heart Sutra (translation by Edward Conze) we read:

*"Here, Sariputra, form is emptiness and the very emptiness is form; emptiness does not differ from form, form does not differ from emptiness; whatever is form, that is emptiness, whatever is emptiness, that is form, the same is true of feelings, perceptions, impulses and consciousness".*

**The Buddhist understanding of emptiness is different from the common meaning of being empty of something or containing nothing and it is definitely not intended as 'non-existence' in the nihilistic sense of nothingness at all.** We could substitute the term 'emptiness' with oneness, openness, timelessness or 'pure potentiality' and the term 'form' with diversity, manifestation, display, play of effulgence or adornment.

**Emptiness, the essential potentiality of Pure Being can and does manifest as forms, feelings, perceptions, impulses and consciousness and these are and remain pure and without characteristics just like 'magical illusions',** not separate from their essential pure source. The two poles of emptiness and form don't exclude each other; on the contrary they are actually just two modes of being of the same Timeless Mind varying in degree.

**Reality or Mind is an expanse of 'infinite potentiality' which expresses itself in various illusory (empty and pure) 'magical forms' which are 'non-definable' and non-separate from one another and their source.** Ultimately, individual beings are an infinite and ceaselessly occurring display within the indivisible empty and pure potentiality of Timeless Being beyond one or many.


## The Principle of Polarity in Buddhist Tantra

In Tantric Buddhism, within the highest form of Tantra, we find the Principle of Polarity (and Vibration) expressed in the transformation of the five types of 'impure' emotions (anger, greed and attachment, dullness, envy and pride) which bind sentient beings to endless rebirth in Samsara, into the five aspects of pure Wisdom characteristic of Nirvana, or Awakened Awareness.

This is achieved by employing various Enlightened Deities as symbols of the pure and non-dual manifestation of the energy of Reality which, when not recognized and therefore experienced dualistically within the frame of subject and object, acts as a fuel for the five types of disturbing emotions.

**Since the ground energy of Pure Being behind both the 'impure' emotion and the 'pure' Wisdom comes from the same source which is the potentiality of Mind, it is possible to transform one into another first and finally transcend both poles and integrate oneself into this pure potentiality (of Mind) itself, experiencing oneself as the timeless center of one's dimension and, at the same time, as the totality of all phenomena (the Universe in terms of microcosm and macrocosm).**

Ultimately, Samsara, as the limited awareness of unenlightened experience of a sentient being and Nirvana as

Timeless Awareness of Pure Being, are like the two **inseparable** poles of the same potentiality of Timeless Ground of Pure Being.

75

*Do not harm others*

*Practice virtue and benefit others*

*Tame your own mind*

*This is the Teaching of the Budda*

# Chapter 6

# The Principle of Rhythm (or Cyclicity)

*"Everything flows, out and in; everything has its tides; all things rise and fall; the pendulum-swing manifests in everything; the measure of the swing to the right is the measure of the swing to the left; rhythm compensates."*

*The Kybalion*

The Principle of Rhythm embodies the truth that everything in the physical, mental and spiritual dimensional planes  express itself in rhythm from action to reaction, from activity to inactivity with a to-and-from movement, a flow and inflow, out and in, a swing forward and backward, an advance and a retreat, a rising and a sinking, a giving and a receiving. **The very essence of the play of Reality itself is always a spontaneous outpouring and an in drawing of energy and manifestation.**

The Principle of Rhythm or Cyclicity is connected to the Principle of Polarity described in the previous chapter and it usually manifests between the two poles described therein. **The swing of Rhythm is not necessarily to the extreme poles, but simply toward first one pole and then the opposite one in varying levels and degrees.**

We can observe this principle in the creation and destruction of worlds and universes, the rise and fall of the tides, in the rise and fall of nations and cultures, in the life history of all things and living being on earth, the beating of the human heart and the breathing in and out of the lungs, **and especially in the mental states of sentient beings.**

This rhythmic motion is not necessarily always in a straight line; in fact these motions are usually in cycles.  **Cyclicity is only a more complex form of rhythm and is dependent on the latter.**

Ciclicity happens when the action and reaction, the attraction and repulsion, arising from the conflict between the force of the rhythmic swing in a straight line on the one hand, and the attractive and repellent forces from without, on the other hand, tend to swing the movement in a perfect circle around a central point of motion manifesting the universal tendency to convert the straight path of the swing into a circular path or cycle.

Proof of this is the movements of small and large bodies in the physical universe, like the electrons around the atoms, the planets around the suns and the galaxies around the universe which perpetually revolve in a circle around some given center point continuing in cyclic revolution instead of falling toward the center due to the Principle of Rhythm and Cyclicity.

**All living things including sentient beings are born, grow, and die, and then are reborn, always completing a full cycle.** And the same applies to all great movements, philosophies, beliefs, fashions, governments, all manifesting birth, growth, maturity, decadence, death and then a new birth. The cycle always completes itself, it's Law.

Also in the mind of beings the succession of moods, feelings and other states of consciousness manifest following the Principle of Rhythm and Cyclicity. In the Tibetan tradition, for example, it is said that if a member of one's family died at a particular age, or at a particular time of year, then at that age or at that time of year all the members of the family are susceptible to death because of the tendency of events to recur in cyclic patterns.

**It's easy to observe how the Law of Rhythm has affected us throughout our lives, how a period of enthusiasm has been invariably followed by an opposite feeling or mood of depression.** Likewise, periods of courage have been followed by equal feelings of fear and so on. For example we can notice that **when we indulge to an extreme degree in a particular emotion or feeling, we have the tendency to fly to the opposite pole of that feeling or emotion.**

In fact it's only normal to feel these 'ups and downs' as an expression of the Law of Rhythm, and we shouldn't aim at becoming like a stone, but as we will learn in chapter eight, an understanding of the workings of this principle, will give one the key to the mastery of these rhythmic swings of feelings and moods, and will enable one to come to know oneself better in order to avoid being carried away so easily by these 'ups and downs'.

**We will also learn how the only escape from Cyclicity is found in the process of transmutation into a spiral movement, and this is accomplished by advancing the central point of motion.** On a universal scale the central point is advanced in the cosmos spontaneously by the Will of Reality urging forward the entire cosmic process, and thus converting the cyclic trend into a spiral trend, onward and upward, in advancing and rising circles toward progression, but even this progression is then reversed backward to its starting point with a process of regression and so on '*ad infinitum*'.

**That's why any real permanent advancement can only be achieved by an individual transmutation of Ciclicity into a spiral movement by advancing the central point of motion by the individualized Will of Mind,** and while apparently traveling around in perpetual circle, like the average person, one will find oneself at a stage higher at each turn of the cycle in a spiral path to self-realization. When the perpetual cycle of same old events and mind patterns is transformed into a spiral movement, then real progress is possible. **But this is not easy task, as the vast amount of old primary causes producing the same effects try to beat us down like a hammer on a pin.**

# The Principle of Rhythm in Buddhism

The Principle of Rhythm in Buddhism is expressed by the concept of 'impermanence' and also by the ultimate state of Enlightenment of a 'fully Awakened One'. In Buddhism, in His first teaching after His Enlightenment, the Buddha laid out the proposition of the Four Noble Truths. One of these four Truths is the truth of suffering which is connected to impermanence stating that '*all compounded things are impermanent*'.

**Here compounded means all that is not indivisible, in other words all that can be known in terms of subject and object is impermanent.** The truth of the impermanence of phenomena is another aspect of the Law of Rhythm which expresses always a flow and inflow, a swing forward and backward, an advance and a retreat, **nothing is stable and nothing remains the same, all is in motion, all is impermanent.**

On the physical level, the birth and death of universes and the inhabiting beings is always found to be in cyclic trends as part of the impermanence of all phenomena.

**At the level of mind, Buddhism explains that there is always an empty gap of stillness between the movement of thoughts or 'strings of thoughts' which we call concepts, and that these two modes of mind's manifestation, stillness and movement, alternate in rhythmic fashion.**

On an ultimate level, at the level of Enlightenment, the Principle of Rhythm is expressed in the activities of a fully Awakened One, emanating for the benefit of others (without ever leaving the Knowledge of the Pure Ground of Being) and returning back to the Ground of Pure Being of mere potentiality in a ceaseless and timeless play of dissolution and expansion.

## The effect of compensation or counterbalance

Since Rhythm compensates we can observe that the measure of a short swing in one direction, is compensated or counterbalanced by short swing in the opposite direction, while a long one invariably means a long swing in the opposite direction.

Everything, in fact, is set off and offset by other things; there is always a check and a countercheck in every manifestation, on every plane of existence. For example, the regular and uniform movement of the planets around the sun is made possible only through the operation of the counterbalancing forces of centrifugal and centripetal gravity, the former manifesting in the tendency of the planet to fly from the central point, and the latter manifesting in the tendency of the planet to move toward the central point, the sun.

**In the same way there are always two phases of energy which oppose and counterbalance each other, one tending to build up, and the other tending to tear down.** All through living nature is this same effect of counterbalance at work, every living being lives dependent upon other living beings, each according to its kind, the very breathing of humans, animals and plants tend to support each other's life.

Humans and most animals breathe in oxygen in order to survive, and breathe out carbon dioxide, but at the same time, plants, under the action of the sun's rays, break up the carbon dioxide, absorbing it and releasing the oxygen needed for humans to survive.

Our mental states are subject to the same rule; we can observe that the person who is able to feel great joy is also subject to strong suffering while the one who feels little pain is only capable of feeling little joy and so on. **The temperaments which only permit a low degree of enjoyment afford an equally low degree of suffering, and vice versa.**

The capacity for pain and pleasure in each individual being is in balance as the effect of the Law of Rhythm. It is sometimes said that one has to 'pay the price' of anything he possesses or lacks or that everything has a kind of price in one's life as the effect of compensation. **In fact compensation means that the appearance of a given amount of energy somewhere entails the disappearance of the same amount somewhere else, and so we can observe that we can get only what we give.**

This is true, as **there is nothing furnished for free, nothing given for nothing in the Universe, the equivalent is always demanded and rendered, another manifestation of the Law of Cause and Effect.**

**Moreover, everything has its pleasant and unpleasant sides, whatever one gains seems to be paid for by the things that one loses.** Every excess causes a defect, every defect an excess, every faculty which is a receiver of pleasure has an equal penalty put on its abuse, every sweet has its sour, and vice versa.

Examples would be virtually infinite and each one can find it at work by looking back at the course of one's life and the lives of those around. The effect of compensation of the Law of Rhythm and the Law of Cause and Effect are always in operation, bringing into balance and counter-balancing every aspect of existence, even though several lives may be required for the return swing of the pendulum of Rhythm to manifest in one's life.

The Hermetic teachings admit to the truth of rebirth as a chain of lives experienced by each sentient being. Lifetime after lifetime each sentient being experiences a succession of events which unfold as projections of one's Timeless Mind just as dreams unfold in one's consciousness during a single night's sleep.


## The Principle of Cyclicity: 'Samsara', perpetual wander and rebirth in the Western and Eastern spiritual traditions

**The word 'Samsara', literally meaning 'continuous flow' or 'perpetual wander',** is the repeating cycle of birth, life, death and rebirth found, although expressed in different ways, within

Hinduism, Buddhism, Taoism, Tibetan Bön, Jainism, and to some extent in Sikhism.

The followers of the Kabala also believe in the reincarnation of souls (Gilgul), and in ancient Greece, Orphism, Pythagoras, Plato and Socrates spoke about the 'metempsychosis' or the transmigration of souls. **Early Christians believed in the transmigration of souls before the second council of Constantinople in A.D. 553, declared it a heresy.**

Although we find reincarnation in most spiritual traditions around the world, **each of these traditions holds a slightly different view,** for example Jainism and some Hindu texts maintain that one who performs extremely evil actions can also be reborn as a plant or a mineral. On the other hand, most schools of Hinduism and Buddhism maintain that plants and rocks cannot be included in the cycle of possible rebirths since they lack the possibility of experience and volition necessary to produce the causes to further rebirth.

Whether this is true or not is a subject of debate also within modern science, **however in the Hermetic Teachings plants and minerals are considered included within the Mind's Principle, and therefore maintaining a very 'rudimentary' type of 'mindness'.**

In the Buddhist Teachings the process of rebirth is precisely explained in details and in Buddhism it is stated that the stream of consciousness upon death or more precisely the dissolution of the five aggregates (form, sensation, perception, karmic formations and consciousness) become one of the contributing factors, along with the totality of all karmic causes planted in the all ground consciousness, (see chapter one for an explanation of this consciousness), for the arising of a new aggregation and a new set of consciousness and personality in the next birth.

**The death of one identification with an individual self-grasped personality becomes the contributing cause for the arising of a further identification with another self-grasped personality.** The consciousness of the new being is neither identical nor entirely different from that of the deceased **but the two forms a causal continuum or stream.**

The fundamental cause of 'compulsory' rebirth **is the not knowing, or ignorance of the real nature of Reality and the potentiality of Mind to manifest as a play of forms, followed by the subsequent identification with what is manifested in a dualistic manner of subject and object**, giving rise to infinite self-grasped identifications and karmic formations within time and space.

When ignorance of the Timeless nature of Pure Being is uprooted, through non-dual Wisdom, rebirth ceases or is manifested willingly or, to be more precise, spontaneously to benefit beings trapped in self-inflicted rebirth or 'Samsara'.


## Does Samsara, relative time and space have a beginning and an end?

Time and space are relative concepts as there is no such thing as time to be found somewhere in space, only a personal relative experience of it. **Creation is timeless but the personal experience of a portion of creation is in time and space.** Just like the objects reflected on a mirror's surface do not appear in space and time but are contained evenly on its surface, all of Mind's potentiality of manifestations are in their true nature completely beyond the measure of time and space but appear as they do in the Timeless Expanse of the pure 'Now' of Mind as illusory events within space and time.

**Enlightened experience of Reality is beyond time and space but has free and spontaneous access to what is manifested in time and space, transcendent and immanent at the same time.** All relative possible experiences of infinite past, present and future events can be known in Awakened experience as a potentiality of infinite possibilities of events and meanings.

The Dzogchen Tantra text 'The all creating king' in this regard says:

*"The three times are a single one without distinction. Arising is primordial, with neither before nor after. Because Reality (Dharmakaya) is one and completely all-pervading, one rests within the nature of the greatest of the great".*

The Hindu teachings call it God's infinite dreams, and a great Hindu Teacher once said that God needs sentient beings to know itself. In the Hermetic teachings the whole of creation is already manifested in the timeless experience of pure potentiality of infinite possibilities ever transforming as energy manifestations.

**In Buddhism it is often said that Samsara has no beginning (as a mass event) but can have an end individually, (not as a mass experience), in fact universes and races of beings are born and disintegrate according to the Law of Rhythm, resembling the birth and death of cells, planets and galaxies without end, 'ad infinitum'.**

In the extremely profound Buddhist Dzogchen Teaching on the other hand, the cycle of birth in time and space has an individual 'beginnigless-beginning' in each moment of non-recognition **by and of the Primordially Pure Ground of Being effulgence and manifestation  as one's own Reality followed by the grasping and apprehension at a dichotomy of subject and object (self and other).**

This process ends at the moment of permanent self-recognition by and of the Ground of Being (each individual real nature) as one's own Reality of Pure Being and one's own  self manifestations as the totality of all potential events and meanings.

Regarding the mass experience of beings in time and space, in Buddhism, the  basic unit of time measurement is what is called a 'mahākalpa' or 'great eon' subdivided into four 'minor kalpas' or 'eons', each distinguished from the others by the stage of evolution of the universe during a particular eon (formation, duration, dissolution and nothingness). During the period of duration of a given universe, the lifespan of human beings as a race spans from 'incalculable' to an average of 10 years **up and down according to**

**the Law of Rhythm for 20 cycles**, after which the period of dissolution of the universe begins and so on *'ad infinitum'*.

While one universe is forming another might be in the phase of dissolution and so on. **What causes a specific universe to manifest as a collective experience is the collective karmic causes, or the sum of all thoughts, emotions and actions of all the beings inhabiting that specific universe.**

On the other hand, as we have seen,  for **each individual sentient being the experience of 'Samsara' begins in the potentiality of the Timeless vast Expanse of Pure Being which continuously and spontaneously manifests  itself as a play of forms and sounds, at which point two possibilities open up:** self-recognition and realization as Reality, the all-pervasive Awareness of the Expanse of Pure Being and total freedom, omniscience and bliss; or self-bondage into a subject-object dreamlike illusory experience in time and space which has no limits in time, it can stretch *'ad infinitum'*.

**Realization unveils its illusory nature and releases the individual cognition into total and permanent freedom as the totality of Pure Being with the possibility to manifest illusory forms in time and space for the benefit of those still self-imprisoned in Samsara.**

Even when Enlightenment and Liberation from rebirth is achieved, the Principle of Rhythm always manifests as an outpouring and an in drawing of light, energy and self-manifestations for the benefit of those who are still 'self-imprisoned' to endless birth and death (Samsara).

# Chapter 7

# The Principle of Gender

*"Gender is in everything; everything has its Masculine and Feminine Principles; Gender manifests on all planes."*

*The Kybalion*

**Mind, the potentiality of Pure Being, is beyond any dualism of Gender, therefore God, Mind, Pure Being or Enlightened Beings are also completely beyond Gender, nonetheless Mind's Timeless spontaneous manifestations appear and manifest according to the Principle of Gender.**

This Hermetic Principle states that there is gender manifested in everything, **the masculine and feminine principles are present and active in all phases of the manifestation of the play of Reality and on every plane of phenomenal existence.** In this case we must make a clear distinction between gender, in the Hermetic sense, and sexual gender in the ordinary use of the term.

The word Gender mentioned in this Principles has a much broader and more general meaning than the term sexual gender, since the latter refers only to the physical manifestation of male and female sentient beings and is one manifestation of the Principle of Gender on the physical plane of organic life. **However, the Principle of Gender as a whole is responsible for the creating, producing, generating and manifesting phenomena on every plane of manifested reality.**

One example in the physical world, is the atom which is composed of a dense central nucleus composed by a mix of positively charged protons and neutral neutrons surrounded by a cloud of negatively charged electrons.

Sometimes we can find the masculine principle identified with the positive pole and the feminine with the negative pole of energy and this may give rise to confusion. The so-called negative pole is really the pole in and by which the generation or production of new energy is manifested therefore there is nothing 'negative' about it on the contrary **we can consider it the mother principle of the manifestation of energy on all levels.**

The function of the male principle is that of directing energy toward the feminine principle, and thus triggering into activity the creative processes, but it is the feminine principle the one doing the active creative work and this is observed on all planes of phenomena.

Arising from the operation of the Principle of Gender on the plane of material energy, all the phenomena of light, heat, electricity, magnetism, attraction, repulsion, chemical affinity are manifested. **The law of gravity is also another manifestation of the Principle of Gender, which operates in the direction of attracting the masculine and the feminine energies to each other.**

Neither the masculine nor the feminine is capable of operating energy without the assistance of the other counterpart, and in general, all forms of life manifest both genders in different levels and degrees. For example each female human being contains male elements and vice versa. **In some forms of life, the two principles are also combined in the same organism in even levels and degrees.**


## The mental Gender

Even though Timeless Mind itself is beyond any Gender, the Hermetic teachings say that Mind's offspring, in the form of consciousness operates through the Principle of Gender.

According to the Principle of mental Gender, Mind's potentiality of manifestation within consciousness operates on the basis of a masculine aspect which for convenience we can call the 'I' and a feminine aspect which for convenience we can call the 'Me' operating in unison.

**According to this principle, the feminine 'Me' is the part of consciousness in which thoughts, ideas, emotions, feelings, desires and intuitions may be produced.** It can be considered as the 'mental womb' capable of generating a mental offspring. This feminine part of consciousness brings with it a realization of an enormous capacity for mental work and creative ability. But even though Its powers of creative energy are enormous it seems that it must receive some form of direction from either its own masculine 'I' companion, or else from some other external mental 'I' to produce its mental creations.

The masculine 'I' on the other hand is able to 'will' the feminine 'Me' aspect giving it a kind of direction and purpose and it is also able to stand aside and witness the mental creations. **These two aspects could also be called the 'the feminine emotive pole', manifesting desire, feelings, emotions and intuitions and the 'masculine motive pole' manifesting will power in order to move, concentrate, restrain, control and act.**

The tendency of the mental feminine principle is always in the direction of receiving impressions, while the tendency of the masculine principle is always in the direction of giving them out. **The feminine principle is responsible for the work of generating new thoughts, concepts, ideas, including the work of imagination and intuition. The masculine principle contents itself with the work of willing and directing** and yet without the active help of the masculine principle, the feminine principle can become content with generating mental images which are sometimes the result of impressions received from the will of other minds, instead of producing original mental creations.

**I cannot overstress that both male and female sentient beings operate through both mental genders and neither of them can function without the other counterpart.**

The feminine is found in the work of active mental generation, and the masculine in the form of willing, stimulating and directing the creative portion of the mind.

The normal mode of operation for both the masculine and feminine mental principles is to co-ordinate and act harmoniously in unison, but unfortunately sometimes the masculine mental principle becomes too lazy and **the consequence is that one can become easily ruled and 'hypnotized' by the minds and wills of others, accepting thoughts and ideas instilled into the 'Me' from the 'I' of others.** The reason for this is that mental influence and suggestion operates along the lines of the feminine desire force and masculine will power employed generally in combination.


## The phenomena of mental suggestion

In the phenomena of mental induction and suggestion, a combination of will power and desire force, the two aspects of Mind's manifesting power, may be used.

Will power may be used to either awaken the desire force in another person or to subjugate the other person's will. Likewise desire force can either be used to induce a similar desire in another person or to charm and captivate the other person's will.

Desire force acts in the direction of drawing, pulling, attracting, and charming, while 'will power' acts in the direction of compelling, forcing, driving, and demanding. Desire always draws its object toward itself while the will always overpowers and compels its object, generally in the sense of driving it into action.

**Most people and sentient beings in general use both of these aspects somewhat unconsciously and haphazardly with very little results,** but, just like any other skill, they can also be mastered consciously and when used unscrupulously and unethically they can be  responsible for all the phenomena of mental influence, fascinations, suggestions, hypnotism, and en masse manipulation.

**The induction of mental states in others by means of suggestion has to do entirely with the feeling phase of the mind, since it deals with the production of 'emotional states' rather than 'rational mentality'.**

This is usually done by using a combination of **both** will power and desire force in the following way:

- **Will power is used in the form of 'authoritative suggestions', assertions and assumption and by inducing feelings in the hearer arising from the accepted statements, without resistance and without any attempt to submit the matter to self-judgment and reason.** This can also be done through multiple repetition of the asserted statement as a given fact. One example is the phenomena of hypnotism, where suggestion is the active factor and the hypnotic passive condition is the psychological state in which the effect of suggestions is heightened. In the phenomena of hypnotism the will of the subject is overpowered by the will of the practicing hypnotist and the various suggestions are then made to him. In this undesirable 'weakened state of will' the most absurd suggestions are accepted and acted upon, the most extraordinary delusions are entertained, and the suggestions for future actions are made effective. One should never get hypnotized.

- **Desire force, on the other hand, is used in the form of charming and awakening specific emotions in the hearers in order to obtain a specific aim.** A typical example of the operation of this form of mental suggestions through desire force is employed by skillful politicians, religious and spiritual leaders, salesmen, advertising agents, lawyers etc. They do this by using words which are symbols for deep feelings and emotions, knowing that these 'word symbols' if spoken with the proper tone and expression, will induce the mental images, feelings and emotions which they represent in the subconscious minds of the hearers. The desired emotions are aroused through the use of symbols and induced mental images. The emotions, whether it is love, fear, hate, desire, patriotism, courage, jealousy, or sympathy, are awakened by the skillful use of words, tones, and expressions which act as symbols for clear mental images and strong feelings. In this sort of phenomena the content and the logic behind is often not important as the feelings and emotions triggered in the subconscious minds of the hearers though induction and mental images.

**In a nutshell mental suggestions operate through the Principle of mental Gender by the use of will power and desire force and by conveying a symbol associated with the mental image and the feeling to be induced in the hearer.** Mental suggestions may be either in a form of a subtle insinuation or a bold positive statement, **but they are never in a form of a rational argument or through a process of rational proof.** The same mental qualities that make a 'bad person' strong and powerful will make a 'good person' great, strong and powerful, and in the degree of 'strength' will be the degree of influence, for good or evil, that such person will manifest, remembering always that the true nature of the individual is always the *'total universal goodness'* of the Expanse of Pure Being (beyond the relative manifestation of good and evil).

**By one becoming aware of how the Principle of mental Gender functions one is able, by using a few simple methods outlined in chapter eight, to protect one's subconscious mind from external impulses which are not in accord with one's best interest, desire and well-being.**


## The Principle of Gender in the Bible book of Genesis

*"So God created mankind in his own image, in the image of God he created them; male and female he created them".*

*Genesis 1:27 (NIV)*

We have seen how the Bible is an Hermetic book of symbols, where the inner and secret meaning is always hidden within symbols sometimes difficult to unravel. In this passage the Principle of Gender is expressed. The potentiality of Pure Being, an all pervading mirror-like Awareness manifests spontaneously as a play of effulgence of forms of the same nature of itself, therefore *in his own image*. These infinite forms manifest as physical, verbal and mental phenomena according to the Principle of Gender, therefore *male and female he created them*.

## The Principle of Gender in Buddhist Tantra

*"This is myself and this is another." Be free of this bond which encompasses you about, and your own self is thereby released".*

*Saraha (8th century CE)*

In the Buddhist Tantric Tradition we find the Principle of Gender expressed in the male and female Deities which practitioners employ in order to purify and transform their limited experience of reality into the total vision of Enlightened Wisdom, Reality itself. The Deities employed in Buddhist Tantra are not the deities described in chapter four, since those beings, although considered as deities are still bound by their limited experience of reality and their ignorance of the true nature of Timeless Pure Being.

**On the other hand Tantric Buddhist Deities are a manifestation of the play of Reality itself, they are beyond any Gender, simultaneously transcendent and immanent, beyond any conceptual reference point of time and space, but manifesting Male and Female forms 'personification' of Wisdom for the benefit of those self-imprisoned in 'Samsara'.**

Although beyond any conceptual dualistic distinction of one and many or male and female, **Enlightened Wisdom can and does**

**manifest as male and female Deities made of pure light as the essence of the five physical elements** (space, air, fire, water and earth) in order to give the possibility to those still bound in 'Samsara' to employ them as symbols of the Enlightened Wisdom of Reality and realize the true nature of Reality or Timeless Mind. **Deities are and remain Timeless 'symbol personifications' of the play of Reality, individual and yet without any separate identity, each one integrated as the totality of non-dual Wisdom, the Expanse of Timeless Pure Being.**

In Buddhist Tantra the male Deities represent the 'Method' aspect of Enlightened Mind or the appearance side of Reality, and the female Deities represent the natural 'Wisdom energy' or empty (identity-less) aspect of Reality, and **when appearing in union they symbolize the non-duality of both aspects of form and emptiness, Method and Wisdom, appearance and empty energy within the realization of Reality.**

Moreover the different forms of these various Deities often represent the form of the being which communicated the Wisdom associated with that Deity as a method for the benefit of those sentient beings inhabiting that specific dimension.

Another function of these Wisdom Deities is that by appearing in the three different peaceful, wrathful and in sexual union forms can be employed by practitioners in order to transform the three main disturbing emotional obstacles of ignorance of the Nature of Mind, anger and attachment into the non-dual Wisdom energy of Enlightenment.

As we will see in chapter eight, one can also employ the method of prayer in order to change one's circumstances and events, and, in this case, the various Deities, objects of one's prayers and veneration, **become catalysts of the all-pervading power intrinsic to one's Mind of Pure Being.** In other words, the Deities catalyze the all-pervading potentiality of Mind, one's real identity, into a specific event in space and time, from the potential to the concrete, and one is able to achieve one's aims in this way, always in harmony with the seven Principles of Reality.

Although these various Deities are considered symbols or methods (the psychologist Carl Jung called them archetypes), they cannot be arbitrarily created nor can they be blended with those of other methods or spiritual traditions.
Each Deity has the precise function of bringing the individual to the complete knowledge and realization of Enlightened Wisdom.

To conclude, just like the Dzogchen Teachings, Tantric methods can only be transmitted and taught **by a Teacher which holds an uninterrupted lineage of transmission and has realized in his or her stream of Being the Timeless Awareness of Reality,** therefore, Tantric Teachings, despite being widely available, cannot be applied by simply reading a book.


*"Because of wind, the unity of water appears as many waves. One lamp, by pressing the eyes, appears as two. All phenomena, in reality non-dual, but dualistically grasped, are like these examples. Therefore, in their duality, all phenomena are appearances of what does not exist, like a dream. They should be known to be non-dual."*

*Kunhyen Longchen Rabjam (1303-1363)*

# Part 2

# Practical applications of the seven Principles of Reality

# Chapter 8

# How to apply the seven Principles of Reality in order to achieve new life conditions and circumstances

*"All things are good for the Individual to use, but none of them are good enough to use the Individual."*

*Hermetic aphorism*

**There is only one power of the Mind and that is free and open to all, it is the gift of the infinite to its finite reflections. To be continuously Aware of one's own nature of Pure Being, is to be completely free, therefore if one were able to recognize oneself as Timeless Pure Being and live within that experience, one would be completely free from all limiting circumstances and all of one's aims, wishes and desires would be 'unintentionally' or spontaneously fulfilled for the benefit of all, oneself included.**

But since this is not so easy for most of us at first, so in part two of this book are going to be described a few useful 'relative' methods that can be employed in order to change one's reaction to life conditions and circumstances on a practical level; **moreover, just like the Hermetic aphorism says, spirituality, religion or any type of science should serve human beings and not make them slaves of some useful but binding concept.**

Obviously, when using these methods one should not expect drastic changes in a short time, one cannot spend twenty or thirty years of one's life building up negative conditions as the result of negative thought-intentions, and then expect to see them all melt away as the result of fifteen or twenty minutes of  right positive thinking and a few creative visualizations. Although this might be possible for a few individuals with a very high capacity, the majority of us have been conditioned for so long by wrong views about Reality and have planted so many causes antagonist to our well-being in our continuum of consciousness that any relevant change will take some time to manifest in one's perception.

**Just like a plant will remain visible for some time after its roots have been cut, but it will gradually fade away and eventually disappear, negative thought-intentions and circumstances will still remain active for some time but will eventually vanish by following the Hermetic methods.**

Even though in most cases past causes will try to beat one down like a hammer on a pin, by following and applying these methods the desired change will follow in due course, as each of us have all the resources and capacities to overcome any obstacle due to our birth right of indivisible identity with Timeless Pure Being, Mind or God.

**Moreover, since liberty or freedom is a fundamental attribute of Timeless Mind, sooner or later in the infinite illusory sequence of time and lifetimes, each individual sentient being will find an irresistible urge to discover one's nature of Pure Being without any forced conversion to a set of religious or spiritual beliefs, dogmas or practices.**

*"And ye shall know the truth, and the truth shall make you free"*

*John 8:32*

## Natural magic and spiritual science

The methods presented in this second part of the book could be considered a form of 'natural magic', the same kind of natural magic which the great Giordano Bruno spoke about, but, at the same time, they can also be considered a form of 'spiritual science' according to the western modern understanding of mind and reality.

**Natural magic because they are based on something which is naturally intrinsic to the individual; scientific because they are based on the unchanging Laws of Mind and Reality.**

They should also be considered as the highest form of natural magic because they don't not rely on symbolic rituals nor on external intervention (apart from in the methods of prayer) but only on one's own intrinsic natural power, which is the nature of Reality.

To call them 'magical methods' should also not be of any surprise, as all modern scientific achievements are also based on a kind of 'scientific modern magic'. In fact, just like by knowing and employing the law of physics we are able to build skyscrapers and rockets that fly through the sky, in the same way, by knowing and employing the seven Laws of Mind and Reality on a practical level, we are able to shape our future circumstances in a way that it may seem 'magical' to an external observer, but which in reality is simply and naturally based on knowing and applying the inner science of Being.

**The basis for this is always knowledge, and in fact, when one realizes how one's perception of reality evolves from one's own potentiality of the Expanse of Timeless Pure Being into one's field of perception, one is free from the bonds of ordinary causality and one can change the inner and the seemingly outer shared perception of phenomena.**


## Hermetic method for discovering Mind

We can only conceive of all pervading Mind as something always Being, although it is not  always generally and individually active, that's why the name announced to Moses by God was  'the One who is' or the individualized 'I AM'.

'I' because it is always individualized and at the same time selfless (without identity), 'Am' because it is always in a state of Being beyond all dualities.

One should not confuse and think that this potentiality of Pure Being is an all powerful self-identified principle,  but instead one should  recognize that the selfless 'I AM' is a Timeless Awareness of Pure Being and  is the central principle which is at the root of all things, it is Life itself.  Not life in particular forms of manifestations, **it is something more essential, it is the 'essential unity of Being' not yet passed into diversity, it is a 'non entity' endowed with infinite potentiality.**

All individual sentient beings are and remain always inseparable from their selfless and all pervading 'Nature of Pure Being' but due to different concepts of themselves, they are displaying only a limited aspect of this all-pervading power.

One method to experience Pure Being, from the Hermetic teachings expanded by the Hermetic teacher and metaphysician William Walker Atkinson in 1909 in the Arcane Teachings and somewhat similar to some traditional Buddhist and Hindu methods, **is to visualize oneself divested of all thoughts, feelings and identification with the body/mind complex, setting aside as the 'not the I' category all attributes and characteristics of ego-self personality.**

By practicing this self-examination, having stripped the ego personality of all possible attributes, it is possible to acknowledge *'a something'*  left, a surd, an irreducible element, an insoluble residuum, **something which, while actually self-experienced, is incapable of being described, expressed or designated by rational terms**, a final algebraical 'X', an ultimate timeless, identityless, thoughtless and all-pervading element.

**This is not an altered state of consciousness like the one that can be achieved through meditation methods employed by some spiritual practitioners or through other skillful psychological methods, but simply the pure, unspeakable and essential Timeless Awareness of Pure Being beyond thoughts and concepts  which is equivalent to all pervading Reality itself.** It is all pervading Mind; it is God, the real nature of all that exists.

By examining the nature, attributes and qualities of this element of 'Pure Being' we are left with *'a something'* which we can be experienced individually **(it is never a mass experience)** but we cannot describe; **a timeless, identityless and complete 'individually self-aware Expanse of Mind'** which can only be defined by the term *'potentiality'* instead of 'actuality'.

Moreover this newly discovered Expanse of Pure Being never fluctuates into separate events (although one's individual experience of it does come and go at first) like the dualistic consciousness which switches on and off according to various circumstances (for example day and night, birth and death etc), it is an even and all-pervading lucid Timeless Awareness of Pure Being beyond concepts and ideas.

## Hermetic method for discovering the Will power of Mind

Another method from the same Hermetic text is to experience the Will or intrinsic power of Mind. One should start by visualizing all space as being empty of all forms and shapes, and containing nothing but pure 'Mind stuff' or Mind's potentiality, a great sea of energy or force capable of setting into motion all kinds of manifestations.

Then one should imagine a tiny center of power being formed in this great ocean of 'Mind stuff', after which, one should see countless and infinite numbers of similar centers of power of varying degrees of activity being formed in this way, each one composed of the same 'substance' as the ocean itself, Mind or Awareness. All these are centers of activity and energy and power in the great all-pervading Mind of Pure Being, **each one a center for itself, and each one having the whole universe or dimension circling and revolving around it.** Due to its y degree of powe and vibration, each center is positive to some (in the sense of more advanced, powerful etc), and negative to some others.

**By visualizing oneself as a center of this infinite ocean of Will potentiality of the Mind of Pure Being in which one lives, moves and has one's Being, one should rest in this knowledge.**

This is the starting point of all the following methods described in this second part of the book, and it is exactly because everything is Pure Being, all pervading Mind, and all-pervading potentiality that we can use all the methods described in this book.

**Therefore we should endeavor to have a good understanding and some degree of direct knowledge of this first principle** remembering always that as long as one grasps at the seeming duality of subject and object of an individual identity in time and space, one will continue to swing and polarize according to circumstances and events without any real permanent freedom.


## How to change one's perception through primary causation or relative first cause: methods related to the Principle of Cause and Effect

*"To commit negative actions and still hope for happiness is to bring ruin on yourself, like someone swallowing poison and hoping to enjoy the experience."*

*Kunkhyen Longchen Rabjam 1303-1363*


**We are usually very busy attempting to change effects, trying to change distressful situations without discovering the causes behind them and make very little progress in life, if at all.**

When one experiences suffering in one's life, one should be aware that this has precise causes that most of the time one cannot perceive nor understand, but in any case one should never struggle nor fight with the effect which is manifesting, because this will reinforce those original causes making the whole process more painful.

**The most important thing in the process of cause and effect is not so much the event itself manifesting which can be joyful, neutral or painful, but it is one's reaction to what is manifesting.** The way we react to any event determines whether we are able to use the event skillfully to our own advantage and therefore as an opportunity to develop awareness and set positive new causes or otherwise become passive victims of our own 'destiny' whether it be good or bad.

**And this is probably the most difficult thing to do for most of us, as we have the habitual tendency to either fight painful events or become attached and addicted to joyful events and circumstances and therefore passive to them.**

For example when some unexpected distressful event manifests in one's life if one reacts with anger and strong rejection one would end up setting in motion new causes for further anger to arise in one's mind first, **which in due time would manifest as more distressful events causing more anger and so on in a chain of events extending infinitely.**

On the other hand if we use the opportunity to practice awareness, patience, generosity, empathy and compassion for oneself and other beings which suffer similar circumstances we would be starting a chain of new relative first causes for our own future joy and well-being.

Likewise if a joyful event manifests, like for example getting very wealthy (everyone wants money nowadays which symbolize relative freedom) and we used the wealth in non-virtuous ways, we would be missing the precious opportunity to set fresh new causes for further and even greater joy and abundance to arise in the future and instead we would be setting in motion a new chain of negative causation with the consequence of future poverty and suffering.

The same holds true for one's birth circumstances, in fact it is evident how some people are born in powerful and wealthy families and then end up as beggars or even suicide, and some others which start from very low positions in society are able to build an empire for themselves.

**We are always free to choose how we react if have enough awareness at the time of the event; always remembering that every life's failure brings with it the seed of an equivalent success, and every adversity brings with it the seed of an equivalent advantage. Unfortunately the same holds true for**

success: it always brings with it the seed of its own suffering if one is not extremely aware. Knowing this, one should focalize in the positive aspect during a momentary negative circumstance, and be aware of the aspect of suffering during temporary happy circumstances.

In a nutshell, instead or reacting aimlessly and haphazardly to whatever manifests as self-perception of events and circumstances always complaining of negative conditions as they have been or as they are, and getting attached to positive conditions like a glue on a stick and always wanting more, one should always do one's best to start new primary causes which in turn will manifest in due time as the desired joyful effects, and this can only be achieved with the use of presence and awareness.

**Now we introduce the concept of primary causation or relative first cause, the power to initiate a fresh new chain of causation manifested by the individual directed to an individual purpose.** Since the power to initiate a fresh sequence of cause and effect it is called first cause, but since it refers to an individual purpose it is a 'relative first cause'.

This is done by stating and visualizing the desired effect as already an existing reality in the ever present 'Now' of Mind which in turn establishes the necessary primary causes for its concrete manifestation. **We establish the necessary cause or causes, by identifying with the imagined intended result.**

Since all causation is actually 'imagined' meaning that the physical cause is always the effect of what is started at the level of mind, we can affirm that the whole physical sequence comes from an unseen cause, which is an act of imagination. **In actual fact, the whole universe is an act of imagination of the Mind of Pure Being and is sustained by imagination.**

When we employ this method of starting a new fresh sequence of causation we should bear in mind a safe general principle, which is that the whole sequence always partakes of the same character of the intention and motivation of the initial first cause. **If that intention is negative, without any desire to externalise kindness, love, courage, beauty, joy, hope,** prosperity and liberty for oneself and others, which are the attributes or expressing power of Pure Being, the negative quality will make itself felt all the way down the sequence of causes and effects and bounce back to the one who has started it.

One should, therefore, never allow one's thoughts and intentions to dwell on selfish purposes, since every 'transaction' must benefit every person who is in any way connected with the transaction, and **any attempt to profit  by the weakness, ignorance, or necessity of another will inevitably operate to one's disadvantage by bouncing back through the Law of Cause and Effect**. As a rule of thumb, one should bear in mind that whatever one desires for others one gets oneself, the law is of unerring precision.

Moreover we should not think of one's intention as contingent on any conditions, nor as an ideal of the future, and here it is important to realize Mind's timelessness and independence of time and space. **By forming the ideal in the ever present Timeless Presence of Pure Being, and maintaining that ideal, we are shaping the relative primary cause into the desired form and therefore we can expect the result to manifest into the physical world of space and time.**

One should also be aware that the further the causation is from the relative first cause, the more it is bound by impelling conditions, and the nearer to it, the freer it is. **This is why when the manifested effect has become visible in the physical world of space and time is somewhat difficult to stop and reverse it**, the 'karmic flood' is in the process of full ripening, therefore the best way is to work at the level of Pure Being, or at least at the level of mind's consciousness according to the axiom of the Law of Correspondence *as above so below*.

# How to start a chain of causation

Certainly one cannot say that the present circumstances are what they are not, as that would be untrue, but, while being aware of the present circumstances without rejecting them, what one can do is to start a new fresh chain of causation by shifting the attention to a relative first cause, employing mental creative imagination and visualization, the power of sound in the form of positive statements and the Will power of Pure Being which is immanent in each sentient being by its identity with Timeless Mind.

One should therefore start by focusing  the attention to a place where there are no circumstances, the Expanse of Pure Being itself, and from there dictate what circumstances shall be, and then leave the circumstances to take care of themselves without the interference of opposing beliefs. **Even better is to concentrate not on particularized circumstances of health, love and prosperity but on health, love and prosperity themselves, the attributes of Pure Being, the real nature of the individual.**

Primary causation has unlimited creative power to start a new sequence of causation, and it is not bound by inevitable effects which would flow from past thoughts and actions. **It is not habitual compulsive thinking which is always bound to prior causes and conditions.**

**Through various methods one works with the imagined effect to establish the necessary primary causes for its manifestation.** In following this method and eliminating from one's consciousness all consideration of conditions which imply limitations, one is planting a seed which, **if left undisturbed, will infallibly germinate into external perception,** remembering always that there is usually a time gap between the cause and the eventual effect **which always depends on other secondary conditions to manifest.**

To give an example, observe the sky on a sunny day and reflect how it could be raining the following day, or the opposite on a rainy day how could one imagine the next day to be a sunny and clear day. The answer lies in the primary causes for both rain and clear sky **which are already there although invisible to the senses.** And so  in the same way we can set in motion primary causes now which will manifest later, **even though from an outside viewer there are no signs of what is about to happen.** One must also remember that it is not oneself which contributes to the efficacy of this method, just like Christ said: *"it is the Father, living in me, who is doing his work."* One should simply create the perfect ideal and comply with the Laws of Reality which will bring about the result.

**Primary causation through  creative imagination,  positive statements or prayer, functions like a sort of magnet able to draw to oneself those conditions  which correspond in kind to the created ideal in a *'likes attract likes'* fashion. *'Thoughts are things'* is the axiom, and the unmanifest becomes manifest.**


## The most important points regarding primary causation

When working with the Laws of Reality one should always remember a few general simple rules that can be applied according to one's capacity and circumstances:

- Since the individual may act on the totality, the result of this action and interaction is Cause and Effect, therefore, one's energy, in the form of emotionally driven thoughts, volition and intentions, become the primary causes for what one will experience in life as the consequential effects.
- One should eliminate any possible tendency to complain of conditions as they have been or as they are, because it is in one's power to change them using the immutable Laws of Reality.
- One should refrain from harming oneself and others in intended thoughts and deeds, and where possible one

should instead be of help whenever possible to create positive causes.

- Constructive thought is always creative, but creative thought must be harmonious, **therefore one should eliminate all destructive and especially competitive thoughts and intentions.**

- Since love, compassion and appreciation are the most positive emotions, by developing appreciation for one's circumstances as a starting point, one is able to advance the central point of motion (see the Law of Ciclicity) and manifest even more positive circumstances.

- **By giving others, whatever one intends to receive or achieve, one creates the secondary conditions for any specific relative first cause to manifest faster in one's field of experience.** Just to give a few general examples, broadly speaking, the cause of wealth is refrain from stealing if one has this tendency and apply generosity instead; health is caused by non-harming any sentient being if one has this tendency and instead try to save other beings lives; beauty is caused by the development of patience toward others misbehavior; the cause of success in any activity is non-attachment to the outcome and refrain from envy if one has this tendency; the cause of being loved and respected is to love unconditionally, respect others and to avoid to cause division and quarrel if one has this tendency; the cause of being listened and appreciated is not to lie if one has this tendency and try to be truthful instead, and, in general, a moral behavior is the cause of a good birth as a free human being or as 'god like' being.

- If one knows of anyone in distress, one should send them thoughts of strength and help, always developing the habit of sending out thought intentions of help and love both in general and in particular. **Especially when one is in distress or suffering an illness, there is no better way of receiving the help of others in thoughts and deeds than to send forth hopeful thoughts to others who may be likewise distressed.**

- **Related to the previous points is the accumulation of relative merit through virtuous intentions and actions**. In fact when one has an accumulation of merit in one's 'ground consciousness' (see chapter on the Principle of Mind), everything and anything positive can manifest and all of one's desires are fulfilled without any effort.

Of course if one realized the Timeless Mind of Pure Being beyond concepts and ideas as one's true identity, and live within this Realization one would spontaneously manifest the *always positive* character and qualities of the Mind of Pure Being and all activities would be spontaneously fulfilled for the benefit of all, oneself included.


## Desire, love, attachment, fear and the spontaneous activities of Pure Being

**Desire is a fundamental natural principle at the base of all human activities and capacities and it can be wise or unwise, positive or negative.** An example of a wise desire is wanting to start a specific activity for the benefit of oneself and others, or the desire to overcome an addiction, a negative habit or an attitude, or to learn a particular skill.

Even the very atoms manifest desire in their combinations within physical reality. **Desire or volition is always manifest, not only in the doing of things, but also in the refraining from doing those very same things.** In fact, those people who make a virtue of renouncing desire, and who claim to have 'conquered desire' are acting in response to a more subtle form of desire, **the desire not to desire certain other things.** Even if one wants to follow a spiritual or a religious path and realize one's own nature of Pure Being, one needs a strong desire to do so.

Unwise desires are obviously those ones which directly or indirectly cause harm to oneself and others and need to be abandoned or transformed into wise desires.

Eventually if one's follows a spiritual wisdom path to self-realization *of and as* Reality, even wise desires will have to be given up for the totally spontaneous activities of the all-pervading Awareness of Pure Being, the *'totally perfect one'*, as these activities are always aimed at the benefit of others and can never be negative (even if apparently so from an outside viewer).

Attachment, and its offspring fear, on the other hand, can never be positive. Attachment and fear are like glue which prevents one from making any real progress in life. Attachment, grasping and fear, **force one to continue in a circling movement, retracing and repeating the same old patterns instead of progressing in spiral movements** and advancing a little higher each time (see methods related to the Principle of Cyclicity).

Difficulties and obstacles will continue to present themselves until one absorbs their wisdom and gather from them the 'essentials' for further growth, but attachment and fear prevent this to happen, and force one to either refuse to give up what one no longer needs or refuse to accept what one requires. **In final analysis, on the most subtle level, attachment and fear in the form of grasping to an illusory duality of self and other, ignoring the fundamental nature of Pure Being is at the base of sentient beings endless rebirth in the perpetual cycle of 'Samsara'.**

Although being an obstacle, attachment has its root in the spontaneous effulgent radiance of Mind's Nature which is all encompassing  love and compassion, therefore it should not be rejected, but accepted and through skillful methods integrated and dissolved into the non-dual purity of total all-pervading love and compassion, which is Mind' spontaneous radiance.

## Prayer and the Laws of Reality

If everything happens according to precise Laws, is there any reason for praying to God, Deities or Enlightened Beings? Yes there is, and in fact **'the method of prayer' is one of the most powerful and skillful method, especially when nothing else works.**
One must understand that the Mind of Pure Being does not change its *'modus operandi'* in order to comply to one's requests, nor does it make exception, **but it does function through well-defined Laws, and these Laws can be placed into operation, consciously or unconsciously, by accident or design and especially by prayer.** It is the operation of these marvelous Laws which have caused humans in all ages and in all times to believe that there must be a personal Being or Beings who responded to their petitions and manipulated events in order to meet their demands.

In reality, when one employs the method of prayer in order to change one's circumstances and events, the various Deities, God or Awakened Beings **become like catalysts of the all-pervading power intrinsic to oneself as indivisible from all pervading Mind,** therefore one is able to achieve one's aims in harmony with the seven Principles of Reality.

**We have already seen how the word God or Enlightened Being means the totality of all events and meanings which can take any form of a seemingly external illusory being** but that in real sense is not a separate entity, now we learn the four important factors involved in the method of prayer:

- The first factor is that although whatever happens in our lives manifests according to unerring Laws set in motion by ourselves, like the Law of Cause and Effect and the Law of Vibration, by praying earnestly and with faith and confidence in the result, we assume the mental attitude of confident expectation, which is one of the most important factor in attaining a desired effect. Proof of this is Christ statements:

*"Whatsoever things you ask for when you pray, believe that you receive them, and you shall have them" Mark 11:2.4* The present tense in this sentence wants us to have absolute confidence that our prayers will be answered to our best interest and that we should feel as if **we had already received what we have asked for as a prerequisite for receiving it.** There is nothing more important than faith or confidence in the expected result. In another statement Christ says:

*"For to the one who has, more will be given, and he will have an abundance, but from the one who has not, even what he has will be taken away" Matthew 13:12.*

Here Christ is hinting at the same Truth, that **we are only able to express in physical reality what we are conscious of being at the level of inner reality of consciousness or mind.** Moreover, only to the one who is already content and can appreciate what he/she already has, more will be given, but from the one who is complaining for the little he/she has, all will be taken away, according to the seven Principles of Reality.

- The second important factor is that in asking earnestly through prayer, and expecting faithfully, we unconsciously develop the mental image in our mind of the conditions desired and therefore we are able to set in motion a primary relative first cause which through the Law of Vibration will materialize our ideals. **In fact faithful prayer is one of the most powerful forms for setting in motion primary causes**. Related to this we could consciously employ the method of creative visualizations combined with the power of prayer.

- The third important factor is that **by praying to what we regard as a holy object we unconsciously develop the qualities associated with the concepts we have of that object.** For example if we pray to Christ, God, or Buddha with the belief that they are the embodiment of love, health, prosperity, wisdom and compassion, automatically, we develop these qualities, which as we have seen, are the natural and spontaneous qualities of Pure Being, and therefore we place ourselves in an harmonious position in regard to the attainment of more love, health, prosperity, wisdom, compassion and all our desires are fulfilled.

- The last very important factor is that as all beings in the infinite universes are not separate from one another but are *individually* integrated as 'the totality of Pure Being'. Therefore we can understand that on a subtle level we all affect one another **according to the interdependence of causes and conditions,** and because of this, **through prayer one can 'receive' help from Deities, Enlightened Beings *interdependently* or in a way that doesn't contradict the causes that one has set in motion through the Law of Cause and Effect and the Law of Vibration.** An example would be that Christ, God or Buddha would indeed 'help' us getting prosperity, health, love and better life conditions *interdependently* **with the causes of generosity, empathy and love we have set in motion** at least at the level of our mind (Law of Cause and Effect) and our confidence in the desired result (Law of Vibration). **Of course it would be impossible to receive 'help' from an Enlightened Being or God if we were to set in motion causes in opposition to what we are asking for or if we placed ourselves in an opposite vibration to our fulfilled desires.**

**In a nutshell, from a 'spiritually scientific' point of view, whether our objects or symbols of prayer (God, Buddha, Christ, gods, angels) exist or not is irrelevant, since when we pray earnestly, associating in our mind the specific concepts and symbols of the qualities belonging to the object of prayer, we develop these qualities in ourselves regardless of their existence or non-existence.**

Moreover, since Pure Being and all those who have realized it are beyond time and space and can take any form according to circumstances, **prayers are already heard as soon as they are whispered without the need for petition and begging.**

Bearing in mind that, since the generic character of Pure Being can be summed up in the words *'always goodness'* (beyond the relative concepts of good and bad), if we were to develop qualities contrary to its generic character by employing certain objects or symbols for one's prayers (for example bad spirits, demons, etc), one would easily be placing oneself in an inverted position in regard to Reality, and, even though some small obtainments might be achieved for a short while through the force of self-centered will power, **primary causes would soon bounce back and one would suffer, in due time, the consequences.** This inversion would be entirely caused by oneself, and not from any change in the generic character of Mind or the object of prayer. The unchanging Laws of nature work with unerring precision.


## The power of concentration and presence of mind


**A general definition of concentration would be *'to bring to a center'*.** Concentration is the undisturbed power of subjective attention over an object of consciousness; therefore concentration is the domain and the best of mind's tools.

Once mastered, concentration is called *presence of mind* and can also serve the purpose of focusing the Will of Mind (the potentiality or energy of Pure Being) for a specific purpose.

Concentration may be developed by practice and many methods exist especially within the spiritual traditions. One example is the meditation which focuses on the breath employed by practitioners of Buddhism and Hinduism, **in fact the term meditation can sometimes have the same meaning as what in the West is known as concentration, or we could also say that meditation is the practice to develop undistracted concentration, or undistracted presence of mind.**

After having mastered undistracted concentration with a physical or non-physical object (for example a flower or the breath), one's focus of concentration will shift to one's **now utterly calm mind or consciousness itself**, mind will be concentrating on mind itself until a state undistracted by any movement of thoughts or emotions is achieved which is then called *'undistracted presence of mind'*, **or the** *'abiding in the present moment'*.

In a nutshell, the whole process of concentration or meditation consists in fixing the attention upon something which can be physical, non-physical, or one's own consciousness itself and being able to hold it there without being distracted by wondering thoughts or emotions.

**Once mastered in practice sessions, undistracted concentration is then carried into all daytime activities and then it is called** *'undistracted presence of mind'*, **or the** *'abiding in the present moment'* **or, as in the words of Eckhart Tolle,** *'the power of Now'*.


## How to develop concentration and presence of mind

There are many different methods to develop concentration and presence of mind, and they all achieve the same purpose.

A simple method would be to hold the mind in a 'one-pointed' way upon an object of attention, which could be a material object like a flower (or anything pleasing to the eyes) or an internal non-physical object **like the breath for example.**

In the case of the breath, one would concentrate in a 'one pointed way' on the inhaling and exhaling process without altering or modifying it. **In case one focuses on an external object like a flower instead of the breath, one should be aware that concentration does not mean 'staring' at something but it consists in fixing and holding the mind, not the eyes.**

By applying any of these two methods, one will very soon start noticing how many distracting thoughts and emotions can carry one away from the object of concentration. **The practice then consists in gently bringing back the mind to the object of concentration over and over again, without following nor rejecting those distracting thoughts and emotions, until one is able to effortlessly direct the focalized mental power of** concentration upon whatever object, concept or aim without any distraction.

Eventually, after having mastered concentration upon a physical (or non-physical object like the breath), one will be able to train in concentration upon one's own mind as an object. **This entails 'remaining' peacefully present to one's own mind or consciousness while staring into empty space, and in this case mind becomes 'the object' of mind's concentration until a totally peaceful, aware and present state of mind is achieved.**

The final result of all these practices is that one is able to carry this new acquired skill of undistracted attention and peaceful undistracted presence into all daytime activities and carry out any activity or task with total accuracy and without any effort, without generating resistance to what is manifesting in the present moment within one's perception.

Regarding this newly acquired skill of undistracted attention and peaceful presence, many spiritual Wisdom traditions fall into the 'trap' of considering the spacious and calm 'ground consciousness' (see chapter one on the Principle of Mind), the 'subconscious mind' as the final aim of their practice and therefore focus on this spacious consciousness, cultivating a calm, blissful and undistracted state of presence **which is then considered a spiritual realization of some form of Enlightenment, when in fact, although a very important acquired skill, is certainly not** *'the truth that makes you permanently free'*, **and not the permanent realization of the totally lucid and all-pervading Awareness of Pure Being, beyond space and time and beyond consciousness.**

Nevertheless, since all the methods of mental imaging, creative visualization, positive statements and methods of prayer are based on the power of undistracted presence of mind, the day you achieve control over the movements of your attention, is the day you will acquire the capacity to change your perception of circumstances and gain control over your life.

**The power to abide undistracted in the present moment is an indispensable quality of consciousness if one wants to make any spiritual or practical change in one's life.**

# Mental imaging and the art of creative visualization

*"All that you behold, though it appears without, it is within, in your imagination, of which this world of mortality is but a shadow."*

*William Blake (1757 –1827)*

**One of the best methods to change one's circumstances and events is the forming of mental images through creative visualization and the Will of Mind.**

If the Universe is in essence a manifestation of Mind and made up of 'Mind stuff' then Mind and its offspring consciousness must have the highest power over its perceived phenomena, and if this is true then **all the so called 'miracles' are just the workings of the Will or power of Mind directed for a specific purpose.**

The power of manifestation through mental imaging or creative visualization employs the three essential aspects of the play of Reality: The potential, the ideal and the concrete.

**The potential is Timeless Pure Being itself, Mind not particularized in any way, not yet brought into form nor thought.**

**The ideal is the particularizing of the potential into a certain formulated thought-intention through mental imaging or creative visualization.**

**The concrete is the manifestation of the formulated mental image into perceived reality.**

Imagination in its positive phase is one the most important faculty of the human mind and lies at the basis of any mental and physical manifestation.

**Creative visualization is simply the creation of clear mental images of the things and conditions desired driven by the Will of Mind, or Mind's potentiality to create and manifest in form.** The creative visualization has the inherent tendency to materialize itself, by building around itself the actual circumstantial conditions corresponding to its mental framework, through a process of Cause and Effect and through the Principle of Vibration and Correspondence.

One shouldn't be surprised by this affirmation; in fact, this is what happens generally in one's life, although unrecognized. Whenever we think in general and especially when we think with intention and motivation with a specific purpose, we automatically manifest in our 'mind's eye' a mental picture of the conditions desired or rejected, although this happens usually without self-awareness and somewhat haphazardly. **The creative power of any mental image is determined by how often you think or imagine it and by the strength or energy of the feelings or emotions associated with it.** The law is that the originating creative Principle of Pure Being in the universal here and Timeless 'Now' creates its own vehicles through which to operate and manifest.

**Therefore when one desires or rejects strongly a particular condition through the emotions of desire, anger or fear, one automatically creates a clear mental picture of the conditions imagined which then tend to manifest in one's field of perception.**

Through strong rejections, feared conditions manifest in one's field of experience just like any desired conditions. **Since we continuously 'think reality' into being in objective perception, the main reason why most of one's desires don't actually manifest in physical reality is the ingrained habit of thinking continuously about the *lack* of the desired condition which will unavoidably perpetrate itself.**

Since the subconscious mind cannot process negatives, even whenever one criticizes, judges and projects negative thoughts and feelings onto others, one subconsciously experiences the negativity as one's own, which in due time manifest in one's physical dimension. This is the reason why one should try to refrain from wishing others any negative motivated conditions, as by law, these conditions will bounce back in due time to its source.

**One can, however, master this process with awareness by following a simple principle: see yourself as you wish to be, and see conditions as you wish them to be, by thinking them out and acting them out, perception will follow accordingly.** You can form your own mental images, through the interior processes of thought-intentions regardless of the thoughts of others, regardless of 'external' conditions, regardless of any environment, and it is by the exercise of this power that you can take control over your own events and perceptions.

If you continue upon mentally seeing yourself surrounded by the conditions as you wish them to be, the creative energy of Mind will group the necessary conditions indicated by the tendency of your intimate intending thoughts.  For example if one desires love, one should try to realize that the only way to get love is by giving love, and that the only way to give love is **'to become love'** or to fill oneself with love until one becomes like a loving magnet. **It is impossible to give love if one doesn't fill oneself with love,** just like it would be impossible to give money if one doesn't possess any wealth.

**The secret of this method lies in the Principle of Mind, (see chapter one) which states that everything is Mind and made of 'Mind's stuff', where the visualized mental image becomes the matrix into which the Mind's Will is poured, and from which it takes form, then finally the ideal becomes the real.**

The method is to start building up a mental matrix, of the first step toward the whole picture, starting with the first thing that is needed, after which, when things have been started in motion, one may add  more details and build up one's mental image in greater detail until it stands out in one's  mind's eye clearly, feeling it as something real, as an actually existing condition in the ever present Timeless 'Now' of Mind, and not as going to exist later on in some distant future.

Things will come one's way, people will appear who are necessary to one's plans, information will come from strange sources and in unexpected times and places, all sorts of opportunities will open themselves up to oneself.  **Of course one must be prepared to act upon these opportunities, as although the forces one has started will supply the right material, one will have to do the work.** The doors will be opened, but one must step in, laziness will jeopardize the process. **The ideal, however, must be sharp, clear-cut and  definite, to have one ideal today, another tomorrow, and a third next week, means to scatter one's forces and accomplish nothing.** If a sculptor started out with a piece of marble and a chisel and changed his ideal every fifteen minutes, what result could he expect?

**To conclude, we have to realize that we cannot create energy, but only transform it from one form to another, by providing the conditions by which the already existing energy can change its mode of manifestation.** By visualizing the desired effect we establish the necessary primary causes for its manifestation. Creation can only be manifested by simply becoming aware of increasing portions of that which already exists as a potentiality. **In a nutshell anything can manifest, because it already is in potentiality.**

**Process of creative visualization:**

1. Start by acknowledging (and if possible experiencing) that everything, including you, is a Timeless Expanse of Pure Being, infinite Mind, all pervading Awareness beyond concepts and ideas and all phenomena is made up of 'Mind stuff'. Acknowledge that the Will of Mind is a great sea of energy capable of setting into motion all kinds of manifestations.

2. Then acknowledge something which is in full physical manifestation right now in your life for which you are grateful, **it's important to start from a feeling of having and appreciation and not a feeling of lack and wanting.** You can only obtain more if you are already content and can appreciate what you already have.

3. Know exactly which further conditions you wish to produce, check that your intentions and motivation is for the manifestation of either more life, health, love, hope, harmony, prosperity and well-being for yourself and others, in whatever projected form you are intending, **knowing that any negative intention in opposition to the general character of Timeless Mind (*total goodness*) would in due time bounce back to its source.**

4. Create a mental picture through creative visualization of the conditions desired, starting with the first thing that is

needed, and adding more details until it stands out in your mind's eye clearly, feeling it as an actually existing condition in the ever present Timeless 'Now' of Mind, and not as going to exist later on in some distant future.

5. **Alternatively, create a mental image and concentrate on the feeling of health, wealth, love and prosperity themselves, the attributes of Pure Being, the real nature of the individual. Give no thought to people, places, or things and leave the circumstantial details take care of themselves;** the environment you desire will contain everything necessary, the right people and the right things will come at the right time and in the right place.

6. Do not strain yourself in holding thought-intention visualization in place,  as strenuous effort defeats the purpose and creates conditions adverse to the desired manifestation. **Try to feel the outcome as a 'something normal', in other words you are manifesting only the attributes or adornment of the potentiality of Pure Being.**

7. Catch as much as possible the feeling of the wish fulfilled, **think from it and not of it**, until you can really feel the actuality of what you desire to manifest. Try to catch the feeling of having rather than wanting. Feeling is thought's life-force.

8. Don't think or anticipate the channels from which the desired conditions will arise, it's not your duty to worry about how the various steps of relative circumstances are going to manifest, **let specific details take care of themselves.**

9. Most important, after the session of creative visualization, if possible, close by returning to the starting point by acknowledging your nature as Pure Being, beyond concepts and ideas and **go back to normal life trying as much as possible to remain present without any attachment, anxiety or fear  regarding the desired outcome of the creative visualization.**

10. Never mention what you are doing to anyone as this will dissipate intention and the energy associated with it and jeopardize the whole process. One should never be arrogant or boastful in general, let alone in the process of manifestation, **always act in the interest of all.**

**If one wants to receive, one has to give first; this is an immutable and universal Law of Being. This is because, by nature, when something is sent out, something must be received, otherwise there should be a vacuum formed, and, just like Aristotle said, *'nature abhors a vacuum'.***

A generous thought-intention is filled with strength and vitality, a **selfish thought-intention contains the germs of dissolution.** Sometimes however, due to negative primary causes and negative circumstances, one is not in the position to give in the field of perceived material reality and therefore one cannot move one's central point of motion (see Law of Ciclicity) and make any progress in life.

**In this case one can employ one's mind instead, through creative visualization and thought-intentions in order to create the necessary causes for  receiving the symbols of wealth, prosperity  and whatever one desires** to live a joyful life which one must then re-distribute for the benefit of all, **thus creating a cycle of giving and receiving.**

**The creative visualization:**

Imagine that you are giving away all the symbols of wealth, prosperity that you'd like to receive and which most pleases you, to the Universe and all the sentient beings it contains.

This could be in the form of money, goods, accommodation, food, clothing, medicines, holidays, innovative ideas, protection from fear, or religious or non-religious charities directed to saving animals or to the poor and destitute and so on. **Strongly feel the sensation of having in abundance all the symbols of  prosperity and well-being which you are now able to give away, and catch as much as possible the feeling of satisfaction in being able to** give to others whatever makes them happy, also imagining that they are happy and satisfied in receiving them.

It is better to imagine you are giving to sentient beings in whatever form, rather than imagining giving to friends and relatives, **as usually this is always tainted with some form of attachment** and it is somewhat easier to do, but you can always include them as well in the visualization.

By employing this creative visualization and volition, always catching the feeling of generosity and prosperity as much as possible, **you will automatically develop the causes of generosity and you will soon find yourself giving also in the material, objective field of experience spontaneously or without much effort**. Not only that, but the feeling of having already prosperity and abundance will also create the necessary causes and 'vibration' needed to obtain the symbols of wealth and prosperity that you desire which will manifest through the Law of Cause and Effect and the Law of Vibration.

**One can make a money magnet of oneself, but to do so one must first consider how one can make money for other people as well, since what benefits one must benefit all, the formula of success is service**.


## Difference between creative visualization and fancy day dreaming

The difference between active creative visualization and passive day dreaming rests upon the simple fact that **in creative visualization the desired condition is thought of as an already existing fact in the ever present Timeless 'Now' of Mind's potentiality** and not as an event which will manifest at some point in the future.

By creative imagination is meant the positive phase of Timeless Mind 's creative faculty, such as what is manifested in the creation of fine literature, art, music, philosophical theory, scientific hypothesis, and so on. On the other hand, **by fancy**

**daydreaming is meant the negative phase of the manifestation of the image creating faculty of mind,** such as the arbitrary and capricious imaginings and fantasies projected by consciousness in a distant future.

Moreover during creative imagination we focus our mind-energy or the Will power of Mind like a magnifying glass for a specific purpose; on the other hand in fancy daydreaming we just dissipate energy without any result. **Do not confuse creativity and imagination with day dreaming which is only a form of mental dissipation which may lead to mental disaster, a waste of time and energy that brings no accomplishment**

## The role of the subconscious mind

**Whatever we desire or intend already exists as a potentiality and it is only excluded from view because we limit ourselves in seeing only the content of our own subconscious mind. Whatever our subconscious feels and regards as true or normal, that is what it manifests to our perception.** Therefore to feel a change of conditions or a wish fulfilled as impossible or difficult to achieve is to impress the subconscious mind with that negative idea.

**Since the subconscious mind is not concerned with the truth or falsity of one's feelings, the best way to impress the subconscious is to assume the feeling of the realized wish or condition desired, by, at least temporarily, detaching the mind from the evidence of the senses and appropriating the feeling of the wish fulfilled.**

Aims and intentions are not subconsciously accepted until one assumes, at least temporarily, the feeling of an already manifested reality, because only through feeling is an idea subconsciously accepted and then manifested in physical reality. Therefore, with the use of symbols, creative visualizations, positive statements and their associated feelings one is able to re-program the subconscious mind and manifest a change of conditions.

**One last important factor to remember is that once a process has started through thought-intention, is very important to bring it to its natural conclusion or at least to conclude a particular phase of it, as by not completing an activity, at least to a certain degree,  is to suggest the subconscious the tendency to never complete anything which has been started** (unless of course one has unconsciously started a negative chain of cause and effect in which case one should stop immediately and reverse the process).

One should ponder well which underlining intention one has and what aims one intends to achieve before embarking on any project.


## Give to receive: The Law of Rhythm and Compensation

As we have seen, the Principle of Rhythm embodies the truth that everything in the physical, mental and spiritual dimensional planes express itself in rhythm from action to reaction, from activity to inactivity with a to-and-from movement, a flow and inflow, out and in, a swing forward and backward, an advance and a retreat, a rising and a sinking, a giving and a receiving, therefore, in order to receive one has to give, it's one of the Principles of Reality called the Law of Rhythm and Compensation.

Since the very essence of the play of Reality itself is always a spontaneous outpouring and an in drawing of energy and manifestation, the same applies to one's own life.

The essence of generosity is a giving attitude to existence; this can be the giving of anything in one's dimension of experience and not necessarily material objects.

In fact in the realm of mind and speech one can always give loving thoughts and helpful and supportive words to anyone in need, sometimes even a smile can be considered a pure act of giving.

This is in accordance with the Law of Cause and Effect and the Law of Compensation, bearing in mind that one should not give expecting something in return as this is unnecessary and detrimental to the spontaneous outflow and inflow of energy manifestation. By giving out one will draw in in a constant movement of energy manifestation without interruption.

Greed, on the contrary, will create a rebound effect causing great strife and deprivation in one's future experiences.


## The Principle of Vibration and Sound: positive affirmations

*"For by your words you will be acquitted, and by your words you will be condemned"*

*Matthew 12:37 (NIV)*


**Words are the symbols of our thoughts and feelings, and a sentence is a combination of thought forms.**

The Principle of Vibration is expressed in statements and positive affirmations of the existence of the conditions which we wish to bring about. **They can help the visualizations to a great degree, and besides have their own hidden power. Just as the visualized mental images are the framework around which the actual material conditions form themselves, the statements in the form of positive affirmations are the pattern around which the visualized mental images form themselves. The positive statement is the effect which is able to establish the relative primary causes for its manifestation.**

One should not say that such a condition will be, because that would affirm its lack in the present moment and give a negative suggestion to the subconscious, **but one should boldly assert the new conditions in actual being in the ever present Timeless 'Now' of Mind of Pure Being, affirming them earnestly and positively, in the present tense, avoiding all half-hearted statements, for they result in half-hearted results.** Statements should be employed preferably in a state of meditation and concentration and never publicly or loudly to other people. **They are one's secrets.**

It is true that one cannot keep evil or negative thoughts from coming, but one can certainly keep from entertaining them. **The best way to do this is to observe them, let them go or affirm their opposite; the best way to overcome darkness is with light, the best way to overcome cold is with heat and the best way to overcome evil is with goodness.**

If one wishes to connect and receive particular positive vibrations in the form of thoughts and feelings from others, one should develop a mental atmosphere or vibration corresponding with those vibrations one wishes to receive, and if one wishes to avoid vibrations of a certain kind, the best way is to rise above them in one's own mind, and to cultivate mental vibrations opposite to them. Since the positive always overcomes the negative, positive mental states always overcome pessimistic and negative mental states.

**One's direct experience and identification with the Expanse of Pure Being, is the strongest and most 'positive' mental state one can produce or achieve.**


## Examples of general positive affirmations

Statements can be combined with the related creative visualization for the manifestation of one's positive aims, **most important one should feel the actuality of the statement and then rest in the newly manifested state of mind beyond concepts or further ideas;** here I will give just a few general examples.


*I am an all pervading Expanse of Pure Being.*

*I am of the nature of Timeless Pure Being therefore I can overcome any obstacles.*

*I am the totality of all events and meanings.*

*I am of the nature of Timeless Pure Being therefore whatever happens to relative reflection of my personality is irrelevant.*

*I manifest an adornment of symbols of joy, wealth, love and bliss in my perception.*

*I manifest infinite life, love and liberty.*

*I am fearless and relaxed in all circumstances and in the face of the Truth of Pure Being.*

*I am and I feel joyful and fulfilled.*

*I can be what I desire and will myself to be.*

*All my wishes are spontaneously fulfilled for the benefit of all, including myself.*

*I'm fulfilled working for everyone's wellbeing.*

*I manifest health and radiate cheerfulness, love and joy.*

*Loving light floods my mind and body, I am and I feel loved and I love unconditionally.*

*I am grateful for all the good things that have already manifested in my life and the ones which are about to manifest.*

*I forgive everyone and everyone forgives me.*

*I am emotionally free and fulfilled.*

*I surround myself with an atmosphere of success in all my activities.*

*My field of experience is filled with manifest symbols of wealth and bliss.*

*I am the health, wealth and love of Pure Being; I manifest an adornment of virtuous qualities in my field of experience.*

*I allow financial freedom and independence to manifest in my perception effortlessly.*

If you have debts:

*I am and I feel debt free, completely free, I don't owe anything to anyone but Love.*

**One should always remember that no matter what the difficulty is, no matter where it is, no matter who is affected, there is no 'patient' but oneself, or one's mind, and therefore one has to convince only oneself of the truth which one desires to see manifested in one's perception.**

## Alternative method of positive affirmations

We have seen how to work with positive affirmations according to the Principle of Sound or Vibration, where one repeats the positive self-suggestion in the form of statements in the first person, using the conscious mind to re-program the subconscious mind.

Now I'm going to explain a different method of working from the individual subconscious mind to the conscious mind of one's personality. The reason for this approach lies in the fact that the subconscious mind is very close to the real nature of Pure Being (although still tainted by a state of unknowing Reality), which lies at the heart of every individual. **In this case, one imagines oneself sitting in front of one's personality and the suggestion is made in the second person.**

Example of positive affirmations in the second person:

*You are an all pervading Awareness of Pure Being.*

*You are of the nature of Pure Being (or God), therefore you can overcome any obstacles.*

*You are the totality of all events and meanings.*

*You are of the nature of Pure Being therefore whatever happens to the relative reflection of your personality is irrelevant.*

*You manifest an adornment of symbols of joy, wealth, love and bliss in your field of experience.*

*You express infinite life, love and liberty.*

*You are fearless and relaxed in all circumstances and in the face of the Truth of Pure Being.*

*You feel joyful and fulfilled.*

*You can be what you desire and will yourself to be.*

*You manifest health and radiate cheerfulness, hope and joy.*

*You surround yourself with an atmosphere of success in your activities.*

*You are emotionally free and content.*

*Your field of experience is filled with manifest symbols of wealth and bliss.*

*You allow financial freedom and independence to manifest in your field of experience effortlessly.*

One can try both methods and choose the one that gives the best results for you as both methods work through different routes but reach the same goal.


## Like attracts like

**Although there are indeed methods, like the ones presented in this part of the book, that can be employed in order to change one's perception of circumstances, the idea of achieving all of one's desires overnight is a misconception based on not knowing clearly the seven Principles of Reality.**

The term 'Law of Attraction' was coined by the great writer, scholar and Hermetic teacher William Walker Atkinson (the author of the Kybalion) in 1906 in his published book '*Thought vibration or the law of attraction in the thought world*'.

**But in that and other books, Atkinson clearly states that the law of attraction and materialization are part of the working of the Law of Cause and Effect in its phase of thought attraction.**

**In fact the so called 'Law of Attraction' is the phenomenal effect or the visible manifestation of the working and interaction of the Law of Vibration, the Law of Correspondence and the Law of Cause and Effect.** This effect manifests in a '*like attract like*' fashion on all planes of mind, energy and physical reality creating the conditions for various events to manifest in the mind first as thoughts and emotions and subsequently in the physical plane of perceived reality, giving the justified impression that things attract or repel each other as they do according to their respective vibrations, causes and conditions.

As we have already seen, circumstances manifest only when the secondary conditions are conducive for that particular event to manifest. **Each one of us is surrounded by a mental atmosphere arising from one's own prevailing mental states, thoughts, feelings, and also arising from the 'thought currents' of other beings which one has attracted to oneself by the effect of mental attraction.** In general, one is more affected by vibrations in harmony with his own accustomed feelings and mental states, than by those of opposite natures.

**The sum of all of one's intimate thoughts, intentions and feelings form a vibration which  is always felt by the people around and therefore it acts as a sort of magnet for what is similar in kind, good  attracts good and repels evil, and evil attracts evil and repels good, fear attracts fear and so on.**

Each living being is continually drawing to oneself people, things, objects and even circumstances in harmony and accord with one's prevailing mental states and feelings. Each individual is also constantly desiring and rejecting what he perceives as external to himself **but which is in fact is only a compatible reflection of the predominant emotional vibration expressed by his mind at that particular time.**

Like attracts like, and the mental states determine what one draws to oneself where the predominant mental attitude serves to attract similar influences and to repel the opposing ones. This being so, if one wishes to receive the vibrations of the thoughts and feelings of others of certain kind, one must place oneself in a mental vibration corresponding with those vibrations one wishes to receive. And, likewise, **if one wishes to avoid vibrations of a certain kind, the best way is to rise above them in one's own mind,** remembering always that a sense of oneness in relation to Timeless Pure Being is the strongest and most positive mental state one can attain.

**In a nutshell *'like vibration attracts like vibration'* in the mental, spiritual and physical world because of the interaction of the Law of Vibration, the Law of Correspondence and the Law of Cause and Effect.**


## Personal positive energy field (aura) and how to strengthen it for personal protection

The aura is often spoken of in Hermetic teachings as one's 'personal energetic field'. **Here it is considered as the energetic frequency of the sum of all of one's thoughts, intentions and**

**emotions in the form of an energy field which functions as a protective, repelling and attracting vitality magnet.**

In the Tibetan tradition, for example, sometimes three types of personal energies are mentioned, which are essential to human life: the 'Sog' or life force, the 'Tshe' or longevity energy, and the 'La' which stands for protective energy. The 'La' is a type of individual energy that is also endowed with a protective function. Usually in the Tibetan tradition if one wants to strengthen or recall the 'La' one needs to receive proper instructions from a qualified Teacher and perform a specific ritual.

**In the Hermetic Wisdom teachings, on the other hand, one can employ visualizations in order to strengthen one's personal protecting energy and vitality,** bearing in mind that the best method of protection is always to maintain an atmosphere of positive intending will and virtuous motivation which will strengthen one's personal power and make the vibration of one's Being function as a protective shield from any adverse influences.

A person whose mind is filled with love, courage and faith may neutralize a multitude whose minds are filled with hate and evil. The reason being that on the relative level of reality the positive pole being of a higher vibration always overcomes the negative pole, because of the tendency of nature to always follow the direction of the dominant activity of the positive pole which is also the spontaneous general character of Pure Being. **The knowledge of one's ability to consciously radiate health, strength, and harmony will bring one into a realization of fearlessness.**

**The creative visualization for personal protection:**

In order to strengthen one's 'personal protective power' one can employ this simple visualization: start by visualizing yourself as surrounded by a distance of about a meter with an egg-shaped field of highly charged positive atmosphere, radiating and vibrating with an intense energy. The important thing is to feel the immediate vicinity becoming charged with 'positive will power'. This type of phenomena is really existent, although the senses cannot perceive it.

If you feel under some sort of mental negative influence, you can mentally form a picture of your aura charged with intense will power reddish-brown in color, flowing outward repelling any adverse mental suggestions that are being sent to you and causing them to fly back to the source.

During the visualization you can also repeat to yourself:

*'I surround myself with a protective energy field of positive will power'*

*'I surround myself with a protective energy field of positive will power which makes all negativities fly back to their source'.*

*'I attract to myself only positively charged beings and repel negatively charged ones'.*

*'I surround myself with an atmosphere of success'.*

**An essential and most powerful statement would be:**

*'I am one with the universally positive Mind potentiality of Pure Being'.*

By doing this visualization every day for just a few minutes with the intention to increase the degree of one's 'positive mental atmosphere' one can develop a powerful tool of self-protection against negative influences.

**The more clearly one can visualize and *feel* the extension of this positive field, the greater will be the degree of positive personal atmosphere.**

## How to overcome obstacles and obstructing negative circumstances

In case one is faced with a sudden negative and obstructing circumstance which can also take the form of an illness due to the power of one's own ignorant past negative intentions/actions or of other sentient beings negative energy influencing oneself, one way to overcome this is to visualize a field of highly charged positive atmosphere, radiating and vibrating with an intense energy and surrounding oneself, repeating in one's mind the following statement over and over in a relaxed and confident way, without charging oneself up with nervousness until a feeling of release is achieved:

*'I deny this negative event or circumstance out of my field of experience, it is an illusion and cannot remain in my field of experience, may all illnesses and negative energy and intentions dissipate, dissolve or return to their source'.*

Alternating this statement with a deeply felt and faithful method of prayer to one's spiritual object of refuge and with a sense of remorse if one thinks might have caused this sudden negative change of circumstances, should, in due time, resolve the situation.

## Character building

Character is plastic, and therefore it may be molded at will using certain methods. For example if you refuse to express a particular emotion it dies out quite quickly. Try in counting ten before acting out a feeling of anger and it dies out, sometimes it will even feel ridiculous.

**If you wish to cultivate a quality in which you are deficient, start by living it as a mental image in your creative visualization and then play the part out whenever you have the opportunity. On the other hand, if you wish to repress a quality, the best way is to cultivate the opposite quality, and the undesirable quality will subside on its own accord,** just like to get rid of darkness you would open the window and let the sunshine in.

Another method is called self-suggestion or self-impression where through the constant affirmation made to oneself, one impresses one's mind with certain ideas, feelings and mental states which will manifest as new conditions in due time.

For instance, if one suffers from fear in meeting other people or speaking in crowds, commonly known as 'self-consciousness', the first thing to do, would be to constantly affirm or self-suggest 'fearlessness' and visualize oneself as absolutely free to do the feared activity, followed by the endeavor to reproduce the outward physical appearance, acting out of the part of the fearless person when possible and appropriate. An example of self-impression in the form of statement could be:

***'I am fearless, I am courageous, I am filled with confidence'***, suggested to oneself in the present tense and always as an affirmation and never as a denial (like for example *'I'm not fearful'*) since a denial would only affirm and suggest its opposite to the subconscious (see chapter one on the subconscious).

Following this principle one would gradually develop into that which one's desires, the ideal will become the real, and feelings will become actions. This rule and example can be applied to the whole line of personal qualities or characteristics; they all come under the same principle.

Since *'like attracts like'*, and the sum of one's mental states determine what one draws to oneself, if one is not satisfied with what is manifesting, one should start by working and changing one's mental attitudes and mental states, and one will soon notice a change gradually unfolding and resulting in things starting to come under one's way spontaneously.

**Self-impression, visualization and acting out the part, can enable anyone to 'make oneself over' in any one of the qualities desired.** Using these methods one would also develop the brain cells in the special region of the brain, associated with the quality, activity or faculty desired until it becomes part of one's personality. **The earnest desire, supported by visualization and self-impression, stimulates the brain centers to manifest the desired qualities, and this causes a more rapid production of new cells and neuro-pathways and the greater development of the existing ones.** Then by acting out the part, one creates a direct demand upon the brain which responds by growing additional cells and pathways to meet the demand, as nature always meets every necessity. **The secret lies in determination and persistency, as repetition is fundamental in self-impression.** Hearing something and impressing one's subconscious mind sufficiently often, tend to become an existing fact, and one is able to act it out accordingly. Constant affirmations and statements made to oneself will soon manifest in actual conditions.

**In the process of acting out the part one should take control of one's physical channels of expression and master the physical expression connected with the mental state one is trying to develop.** For example, if one is trying to develop self-reliance, confidence and fearlessness, the first thing to do is to get a perfect control of the muscles by which the physical manifestations or expressions of those feelings are shown. One should start by taking control of the muscles by which one holds one's head up, with eyes gazing the world fearlessly in the face.

Also one should control the muscles of the legs by which one will be enabled to walk firmly and positively, one should control the vocal organs by which one may speak in the resonant, vibrant tone which compel attention and inspire respect. In conclusion, by getting oneself well in control physically, one will be able to express and manifest any mental attributes one wishes to develop.

Will power could also be developed by taking up the habit of always doing things thoroughly and completely by cultivating stability, decision, perseverance and tenacity. **One must learn to concentrate one's will upon a task and not allow it to be distracted or to wander off until completion** (see the chapter on how to develop concentration and presence of mind). **A good exercise is to learn how to do some particular unpleasant or disagreeable task from time to time as this is going to strengthen the 'mental muscle' which is but another name for will power.**

Anyone can do pleasant and agreeable tasks without opposition or resistance. But it takes an individual with a well-developed will power to do things against resistance from within or without, and **when one has learned to master oneself, one's own**

**moods and feelings, then one will able to master the outside world.**

**Note:** since there are wise and unwise desires, good and bad intentions, one should learn how to distinguish between them and govern oneself accordingly, always aware of the Principle of Cause and Effect.

**Best of all, one should finally realize that the individual is not the personality nor the self-grasped identity, but the individualized and identityless Expanse of Pure Being which lies beyond any 'self-grasping', and that the attributes of ego driven personality are merely adornments that can be worn and discarded or molded at will.**

## How to gain intellectual, spiritual or practical knowledge

Another useful method if one wishes to gain certain information and knowledge regarding a specific subject, is to hold a strong desire that the desired knowledge shall come to one's notice and attention, and at the same time visualize 'mind currents' of thought intentions with a rotational movement flowing forth in search of persons, things, and objects capable of imparting such knowledge or information. **One will soon be driven unconsciously to the desired object of knowledge spontaneously.**

Even more, the adductive quality of thought does more than this, since it seem to act as a sort of 'mentative wire' conveying the vibrations from one mind to another, enabling one to draw toward oneself people who are interested in the same line of work or with similar aims. **In this regard, people thinking along the same lines and with the same desires and intentions, although in different parts of the world, will be brought together in this way.** One will find new ideas or concepts flashing into one's mind, through the medium of all-pervading Mind of Pure Being, or from one's subconscious mind wherein is stored every sense impression and thoughts, or from the subconscious mind of other people who have just released the thought picture of the idea or concept through a conscious intended thought.

**There is another form of thought- intention which, by having a rotational motion spreads out in gradually widening sweeps reaching out further and further each day, according to the impulse imparted to them.** The peculiar feature of this rotary form of though intentions are the movement towards its own center, by which it attracts to its vortex all that is desired. Thought-intention is an active vital form of dynamic energy which has the power to correlate with its object and bring it out of the invisible substance from which all things are created into the visible or objective perception.

**To conclude, by an earnest, firm and confident belief that subtle thought-intention is the connecting link between the infinite and the finite, between the universal and the individual or between Timelessness and form, one will realize all of one's positive aims simply by using the intrinsic power of thought.**

## How to find peaceful poise and master the Principle of Polarity and Rhythm

*"For hatred does not cease by hatred at any time: hatred ceases by love, this is an eternal rule".*

*The Buddha*

The Principle of Polarity in relation to consciousness, states that contrasting and opposing feelings and emotions are in reality opposite poles of the same thing, pure energy manifestation, and that the Principle of Rhythm is always in operation. Now we will learn that by changing the polarity of any given emotion or by rising above it in the free and Timeless state of Pure Being we can work and eventually master the Principle of Polarity and Rhythm.

The first method is to practice shifting the polarity of feelings and emotions at will, backward and forward and thus discover that the feelings and emotions are not fixed and constant but are capable of  being shifted about at will, for example inducing the state of fearlessness where fear has been dominant, or vice versa.

**By shifting the polarity one may change a painful feeling or emotion into its opposite, distressing feelings may be changed in polarity, or balanced with their opposites.** It is in fact not necessary always to shift entirely to the opposite pole of the emotion or feeling, one may change the polarity to its opposite to a sufficient degree **in order to establish a balance and thus create a condition or state of poise, which results in a peaceful state of mind.**

Since action and re-action are equal, one should always manage to have a push or a pull counteracted with a push or a pull in the opposite direction, **and thus maintain a state of balance and poise.** One should never fight or struggle with an undesirable emotional quality by opposing a strong will to it as this would be a waste of energy, and, worse more, reinforce that undesirable emotion.  **Hate is not to be fought against with rejection and hate, as this only adds fuel to the fire of hate, instead one polarizes to its opposite of love to a degree as to find the right poise and balance.** One could also make use of creative imagination and positive statements, by first becoming aware of the negative emotion without rejecting it, and then create a visualized image as a symbol of its opposite, love, and repeat a statement in one's **mind until a state of poise is found.** An example could be, in case of counteracting hate, one would imagine oneself in a situation of harmonious love with oneself and others and repeat the following statement:

*'Loving light floods my mind and body, I'm loved and I love unconditionally'.*

In the same way the emotional states of others may be influenced by polarizing  their  minds on the opposite pole of the scale of the emotion in question, for example **by forming the mental image of love in one's own mind, and then concentrating  its effects upon the other person.**

**There is always a point or poise between the poles of every pair of opposites, but that point exists only because the**

**extremes exist, and in the central point is always found the power of the whole event. At the center of peaceful poise one is able to use action and reaction without being subject to either.**

This does not mean that one should reject one's emotional nature, for that would be rejecting the Will or potentiality of Pure Being. On the contrary, one will find it advantageous to play out the part often, for the energy aroused by the emotions are strongly motive, and will enable one to accomplish many tasks by selecting the emotional activity adapted to the accomplishment of the task at hand, and restricting all other emotions.

**The main difference being that, one is not enmeshed or conditioned by the emotional storms and is able to handle the emotions as a master does an instrument, not giving oneself up to emotions as a passive slave or a blind tool,** but always aware of the reaction and return of the emotional swing of rhythm.

Peaceful poise is true power and it results from balance between all pairs of opposites resolving them into oneness, it is the true state of Pure Being in which one finds a peace unknown to those who polarize to either extremes.

**At the heart of the storm there is peace, and at the center of life there is poise and power, the one who finds the center of oneself, finds the center of the whole Universe, for ultimately they are one.**

**The second and more advanced Hermetic method** would be to rise above polarity into the Timeless peace of Pure Being by adopting and practicing this visualization that comes from the Hermetic Teacher William Walker Atkinson:

Imagine yourself on a balloon which is rising above the surface of the earth into the higher regions of the sky, rising above the lower planes of personality toward the higher planes of Being. As you rise, start throwing off the balloon all your likes and dislikes, loves and hates, preferences for and against anything and everything whatsoever  either good or bad, in short the entire collection of inherited or acquired feelings and emotions and concepts which have formed the body of your ego-personality until now.

As the mental balloon rises higher and higher, **allow yourself to be divested of even the more subtle feelings and emotions, concepts and any identification with an identity, until finally you find yourself divested of every iota of personal character you ever possessed, and rest 'naked' as a new-born baby in the always positive and blissful, Timeless state of Pure Being, beyond any polarity.**

In this way by rising above the swing of the plane of rhythmic emotions to the plane of Pure Being, one learns to value emotions and feelings for what they really are, pure manifested energy, and refuses to allow one's intimate Being to become entangled in them, **calmly partaking at the storm of emotions, without being influenced by it.**

An example of this is the difference between a drop of mercury and a drop of water falling on sand, where, although both touch and integrate with the sand, the former never loses its qualities **but remains pure and limpid without mixing itself with the sand** and the latter, water, becomes entangled with the sand in such a way that it loses its qualities of limpidity and clearness altogether.


## Methods related to the Principle of Cyclicity

*"The flower's perfume has no form, but it pervades space.  Likewise, through a spiral of mandalas, formless reality is known".*

*Saraha (8th century CE)*


**The easiest way to work with the Principle of Cyclicity is to transform the motion of the cycle into a spiral by advancing its central point of motion.**

One evidence of the Principle of Ciclicity is one's tendency to travel constantly 'round and 'round in recurring circles, gradually widening from childhood to the prime of life, and then narrowing to old age and death. **One finds that while the circles are widening or narrowing as the case may be, one never makes any**

**real progress, it is always a constant swing around the same old central point,** a constant traveling which results in one getting nowhere but the old same starting point.

Sometimes one is able, under the unconscious influence of circumstances, to advance the central point of motion to a degree, but since the process is unconscious one can easily swing back to the previous point of motion. **On the other hand by cultivating the habit of constantly willing an advance at each cycle, one will find that though one's life still maintains its circular movement, at each return to a given point one will have advanced a little higher in scale,** just as a traveler ascending a mountain needs go 'round and 'round, each time a little nearer the peak, so will one find that at each circling the old paths will be below oneself.

The turnings of the spiral will get wider and wider so one will have more and more space to find oneself; even though one is covering much the same territory, repeating the same sort of story, **now there is spaciousness in moving through it due to the widening of the spiral.**

By the increasing power which comes from this conscious use of the Will power of Mind to advance the central point of motion to a certain degree at each cycle, one establishes a habit of a spiral progression which replaces the old simple cyclic movement and overcomes the tight grip of Ciclicity.


## Methods related to the Principle of mental Gender: how to protect oneself from mental influences and unwanted suggestions

In chapter seven we learned how through the unscrupulous and unethical use of the Principle of mental Gender by combining will power and desire force (the two aspects of Mind's manifesting potentiality) all the phenomena of mental influence, fascinations, suggestions, hypnotism, and en masse manipulation can be achieved to a certain degree, therefore one needs to know just a few simple but effective methods to protect oneself in certain circumstances.

In general, one should know that people who are affected by any adverse influence against their will, invariably '**believe**' and, above all, **fear** that these influences are effective against them, as fear and belief determines the degree of receptivity to such influences. By their mental states they render themselves negative and receptive to the influences directed against them.

**Therefore the best and foremost method of protection is to assert one's own individuality as indivisible from the nature of all-pervading Expanse of Pure Being (one's own nature) or at least, feel oneself a center of an ocean of Mind potentiality and assume a fearless attitude.**

If one feels under a strong mental influence against one's will or a sudden or unaccountable 'impulse' to do something, **one should pause for a moment, and claim one's individuality at the same time forming a mental picture of oneself as a center of power in the great ocean of Mind's potentiality.** Then one should mentally form a picture of an aura, or energy field charged with one's individual will extending about a meter on all sides in an egg shaped form, repelling any adverse mental suggestions that are being sent to oneself, and causing them to fly back to the source from where they came.

While forming such mental image, one could also repeat to oneself the following statement:

*"I assert my individuality as a center of an ocean of Mind power and Timeless Pure Being. I refuse admittance to unwelcome suggestions and repel all undesirable influences".*

Another, 'more practical' way of protection, is to adopt the habit of **never acting immediately in response to an appeal in form of authoritative suggestions, assertions and induced assumptions until the effect of the emotion induced has worn off to a degree, and then submit the matter to one's reason and discernment, and only then act if appropriate.**

In case of being faced to situations of high emotional intensity it is better to fence oneself off from a too ready response to any sympathetic appeals along the emotional side especially from people that have some sort of social power or are selling a desirable product. If you feel as being carried away by some sort of emotional excitement against your will, steady yourself, raise your will power and ask yourself whether this is a mental suggestion and whether it serves your best interest and wellbeing. **Try to find a state of poise, wait a few minutes and act from there.**

In case you are involved in a business deal of any sort, always beware of any desire feeling induced by the subtle suggestion of words or any authoritative statement made by the seller. **Before buying a product, take a five minute walk and ponder well about the different choices and never react emotionally to any appeal by the seller.**

Also when engaged in sensitive conversations beware that the person standing has the advantage of a certain positive attitude or position, and the person seated below the speaker is forced into a relatively passive position. **Therefore you if ever feel that someone is placing you in a negative or passive condition, rise up and you will feel strong and protected from any authoritative suggestions.** One should be especially cautious, and ponder well before accepting any suggestion if one is worn out, tired, or in a passive or pleasurable state, as that is  when one's will is resting or is exhausted and one is very vulnerable to external suggestions.

In a nutshell, one should guard one's own mind, and also guard one's desire from the influences of others will power, **because through one's desires one's will is called into action.** One should learn how to control one's own will power and do not let it leap into action until one is sure it is right to do so.


## How to free oneself from undesired relationships

Relationships with other beings always depend on the Law of Cause and Effect and the Laws of Vibration and Correspondence. In particular, **the primary causes driven by one's intention that one sets in motion when dealing with other beings will have an effect and shape what kind of relationship one will have with that particular being.**

There are indeed many methods that can be employed in order to 'pay off' one's Karmic (Cause and Effect) debt with other sentient beings. In the Tibetan spiritual tradition one can employ practices like 'Chöd' and 'Sang', but these practices can only be transmitted in person by a qualified Teacher.

On the other hand one very useful and simple method which doesn't require a special transmission and that can be employed in order to free oneself from undesired and painful or abusive relationships is to employ the following visualization:

*Imagine yourself standing up and the person with whom you have a painful relationship in front of you naked sitting on a chair, imagine a red thread or rope that comes from you and is also tied to the other person. Now imagine to cut this thread and both of you are free and happy to be free of the bonding relationship. Imagine the other person thanking you and walking free away from you. Don't mention it neither to the person involved nor to anybody else and repeat it many times until you feel completely free.*

By repeating this visualization over and over one will soon find a kind of release first in one's mind and soon after also in one's perception or field of experience.


## How to free oneself from addictions

Nowadays, due to the skillful use of mental suggestions, assertions and induced assumptions employed by powerful corporations and their marketing strategies, more and more people are becoming addicted to all sorts of products, like medicinal drugs, cigarettes, sugar containing products, alcohol, sex and gambling to name a few. **Since all addictions are based on an underlying craving for fulfillment due to not knowing the Timeless state of Reality and the negative beliefs or habitual tendencies stored in the subconscious mind related to the object of craving,** the first thing to do is to look at the messages that have been implanted into the subconscious mind, because these are the messages that one needs to change.

**When becoming free from an addiction, at the beginning one needs to learn how to simply form a new habitual tendency through will force.** For instance, in case one wants to stop smoking, drinking or a sexual addiction, one will find that three quarters of the entire struggle in getting a new habitual tendency fixed upon the subconscious is condensed in the first week. Here one has to use one's will with all one's might, but once the first battle is won, the whole process becomes easier and easier each day until one is effortlessly and permanently free.

In my book 'Cures Without Side Effects' I've presented a few strategies using natural remedies that can be employed in order to become free of any addiction by detoxifying the organism and supporting the 'PNEI system'.

In this book I will just present a very simple method that can be used in order to re-program the subconscious.

One should start by visualizing oneself in a typical situation but free of the object of addiction and repeat the following statements to oneself:

*'I deny the power of ... (such and such addiction) ...over my free will'.*

*'I am and I feel free, completely free from ... (such and such addiction)'.*

*'I am and I feel free to choose my desires to my best interest'.*

Since the subconscious mind is the servant of the conscious mind and it cannot distinguish between what is real and what is imagined, the important thing is to associate to such 'addiction-free' visualizations and positive statements a feeling of complete fulfillment and freedom from the object of addiction.

# How to help others through the seven Laws of Reality

*"I said, You are gods; all of you are the sons of the Most High".*

*Psalms 82:6*

The best and foremost way to help others is to see them as they really are, reflections or adornment of Timeless Pure Being, just like oneself, knowing that reflections always manifest the same attributes and qualities as their source, all beings are in fact now and always the Timeless Mind of Pure Being.

**Knowing this, if you wish to help someone dear or wish to develop an attitude of compassion, train in seeing others as already possessing the attributes and qualities of Pure Being, in other words, see them as already possessing Wisdom, health, prosperity, intelligence, courage, love and compassion.**

The training consists not seeing sentient beings as they seem to be manifesting superficially and temporarily due to their self-grasping personality because of not knowing the Truth of Pure Being, but to see them as they really are in their fundamental nature, embodying the qualities of Pure Being such as Wisdom, love, compassion, health, intelligence, accomplishment, fulfillment and fearlessness.

You are not inventing a new harmonious 'reality' as a kind of fantasy, you are just trying to see things as they really are; the intrinsic harmony within all phenomena.

The Buddha said in the Prajnaparamita Sutra: *"Not just Enlightened Beings but all the structures of relativity are dwellers in the boundlessness which constitutes the all-embracing love, selfless compassion, sympathetic joy and blissful equanimity".*

Pure perception is never something that happens in the future, but an actuality of the ever present here and now of Reality.

**Therefore if you wish to help someone who is suffering an illness, the best would be to see him or her as healthy; in case of poverty see abundance and prosperity; instead of frustration and loneliness see accomplishment, fulfillment and love, basically try to see the Truth hidden behind the veil of**

**temporary adventitious circumstances.** If this is too difficult at first, the best is to create a mental image of the person you are trying to help possessing these perfect qualities, knowing that the visualized image is a *'facsimile'* of the Truth and attributes of Pure Being.

**Of course this does not mean that one should become uncaring or cold hearted, thinking that everyone is already perfect so why bother to do anything for others.** On the contrary one should carry out all possible helping activities concretely for the benefit of others respecting the Law of Cause and Effect, while, at the same time without contradiction, having the awareness of the perfection of all sentient beings as illusory reflections of Timeless Pure Being.

**One should always remember that no matter what the difficulty is, no matter where it is, no matter who is affected, there is no 'patient' but oneself, or one's mind, and therefore, one has to convince only oneself of the Truth which one desires to see manifested in another.**

## The best and foremost way to deal with life and circumstances

Even though all the skillful methods explained in this book are very useful and can be of great help, one must remember that the ultimate and foremost way to deal with life and circumstances (and of course death) is to become aware of one's own true nature as a **lucid Expanse of Timeless Pure Being** beyond time and space, beyond confusion and concepts, beyond suffering and relative circumstances, and integrate in that knowledge one's existence as a pure experience of the illusory play of Reality, the illusory adornment of Pure Being itself.

# Chapter 9

# Concluding advice

*"The possession of (inner) Knowledge, unless accompanied by a manifestation and expression in action, is like the hoarding of precious metals, a vain and foolish thing. Knowledge, like wealth, is intended for use. The Law of Use is Universal, and he who violates it suffers by reason of his conflict with natural forces".*

*The Kybalion*

In this book I have presented, in a simple and essential way, very profound concepts and principles pertaining to the western and eastern traditions of precious Wisdom knowledge using the text 'The Kybalion' as a framework. I've also explained a few practical and simple methods based therein, applicable to daily life in order to achieve a change in perception and a relatively more joyful, healthier, prosperous and relaxed lifestyle.

Don't let the simplicity of these principles and methods cause you to undervalue them in favor of some more technical, complicated and encumbering modern theories and practices, because in final analysis you will find that the underlying principles of the methods given here is in full operation in all these complicated modern theories and explanations.

**Ultimately, Truth is always found to be simple.** Since, ultimately, each individual is an indivisible manifestation of the Mind of Pure Being one is always merely asking for one's own and therefore one has the perfect right to all there is, always without disturbing or taking from others but with the intention to share and serve others.

**One must therefore always be willing to give something in return for whatever one acquires, since there is no such thing as 'something for nothing' in perceived existence and everything is always counterbalanced by something else. One should never**

**assume an arrogant, imperious and domineering attitude, for true strength and knowledge never exhibits itself in this way.**

While using these methods, and in life in general, one should always remember that every failure brings with it the seed of an equivalent success, and every adversity brings with it the seed of an equivalent advantage therefore one should never lose confidence and awareness in each circumstance.

In final analysis, all manifestations of Reality are the playthings of the 'kindergarten of Timeless Pure Being', oneself, they are good to use and play with, but never good enough to use the individual. **One should never lose sight of the fact that these illusory manifestations are only an adornment of the play of the Timeless Reality of Pure Being;** one must be perfectly willing to lay them all aside when the time comes to pass into the next existence without crying and mourn with attachment and grasping like an infant.

**The 'unrealized individual' thinks that the play of Reality is very real, and therefore that he is not good enough to enjoy it or he needs to grasp at it.** The 'Realized and Awakened one' perceives their unreality and asks for that which he needs from day to day to serve others without fear and without attachment, craving or greed, and when he is called into the dissolution from existence he drops on the floor the worn-out 'toys of this life', and with glistening eyes and confident attitude, marches into the 'Great Unknown' the Timeless Expanse of Pure Being with a smile on his face.

*"Though my view (and realization of Reality) is higher than the sky, my respect for the cause and effect of actions is as fine as grains of flour."*

*Padmasambhava – The lotus born Buddha (8<sup>th</sup> century)*

## Students of Reality

*"Perfection is not acquired in six days, or in six weeks, or in six months. It is the labor of a lifetime. "*

*Charles F. Haanel*


In contemporary western society there is a custom to consider oneself proficient and a 'master' of any given subject  if one has thoroughly **intellectually** understood and deepened the knowledge related to that particular subject, one then becomes a lecturer, a professor and a public figure and gains success and fame.

I'm afraid this very superficial attitude cannot be applied to the science of Reality, the Wisdom Knowledge of Pure Being or to the application of the Laws of Reality. In this case one could only be considered a proficient 'Master' of Reality after having totally and thoroughly realized in the depth one's wisdom Timeless Mind of Pure Being, *'the truth that will set one free forever'* from birth and death.

On my part, I'm still a student of Reality and therefore I cannot claim to have realized nor mastered such profound principles nor the methods presented herein, as, **until the total and unchanging realization of Reality we are all always just students and aspiring practitioners of the Great Timeless Mind of Pure Being.**

*There is nothing to fear but fear itself, you are free now, here, and always and the only chains are those your mind forges for you.*
*Reality is not logical but Magical.*


Om Mani Padme Hum


Finis

# About the Author

Max Corradi is a Life Coach, a Naturopathy practitioner and a musician. Since 1996 he has been studying and practicing the eastern and western traditions of inner knowledge, philosophy, Buddhist meditation, naturopathy and Self-Healing and he has been a student of many Tibetan Buddhist Teachers. He is also the author of complementary medicine and Self-Help books.

To contact the author please write to:

jaborandipub@gmail.com

**Social media:**

You tube: https://www.youtube.com/@noageontology1571/videos

Facebook:
https://www.facebook.com/groups/noageontology

# Other books by the author

Cures without side effects
"Practical healing manual of the most essential and effective
biotherapy treatments"
Jaborandi Publishing

Low dose medicine
"Healing without side effects using low dose cytokines,
interleukins, hormones, and neurotrophines"
Jaborandi Publishing

Healing with Micotherapy
"Self-Healing with therapeutic mushrooms"
Jaborandi Publishing

No Age Ontology
"The Joy of Timelessness"
Jaborandi Publishing

Jaborandi Publishing second edition 2023

For more info write to: jaborandipub@gmail.com

www.ingramcontent.com/pod-product-compliance
Lightning Source LLC
Chambersburg PA
CBHW031253060726
47590CB00003B/880